Presenting:

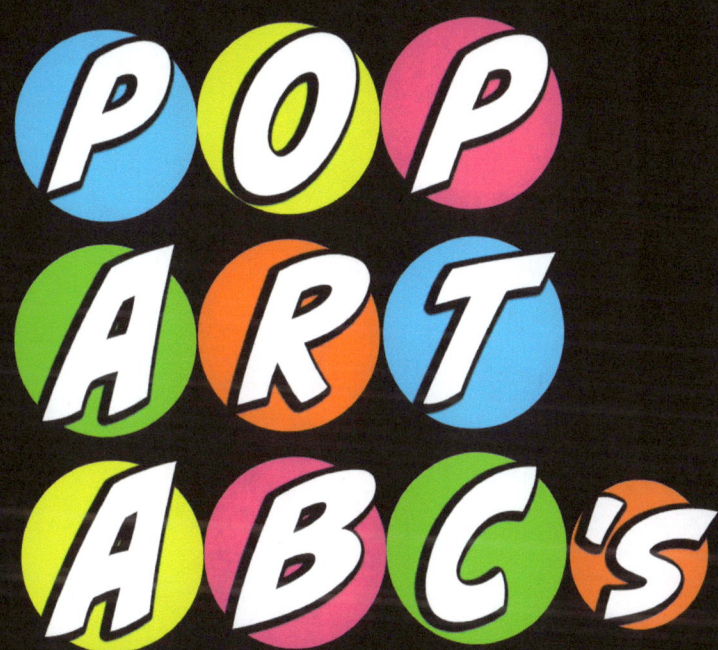

POP ART ABC's

A COLORFUL ALPHABET BOOK

WORDS & ART BY: BRIANNA DAVIS

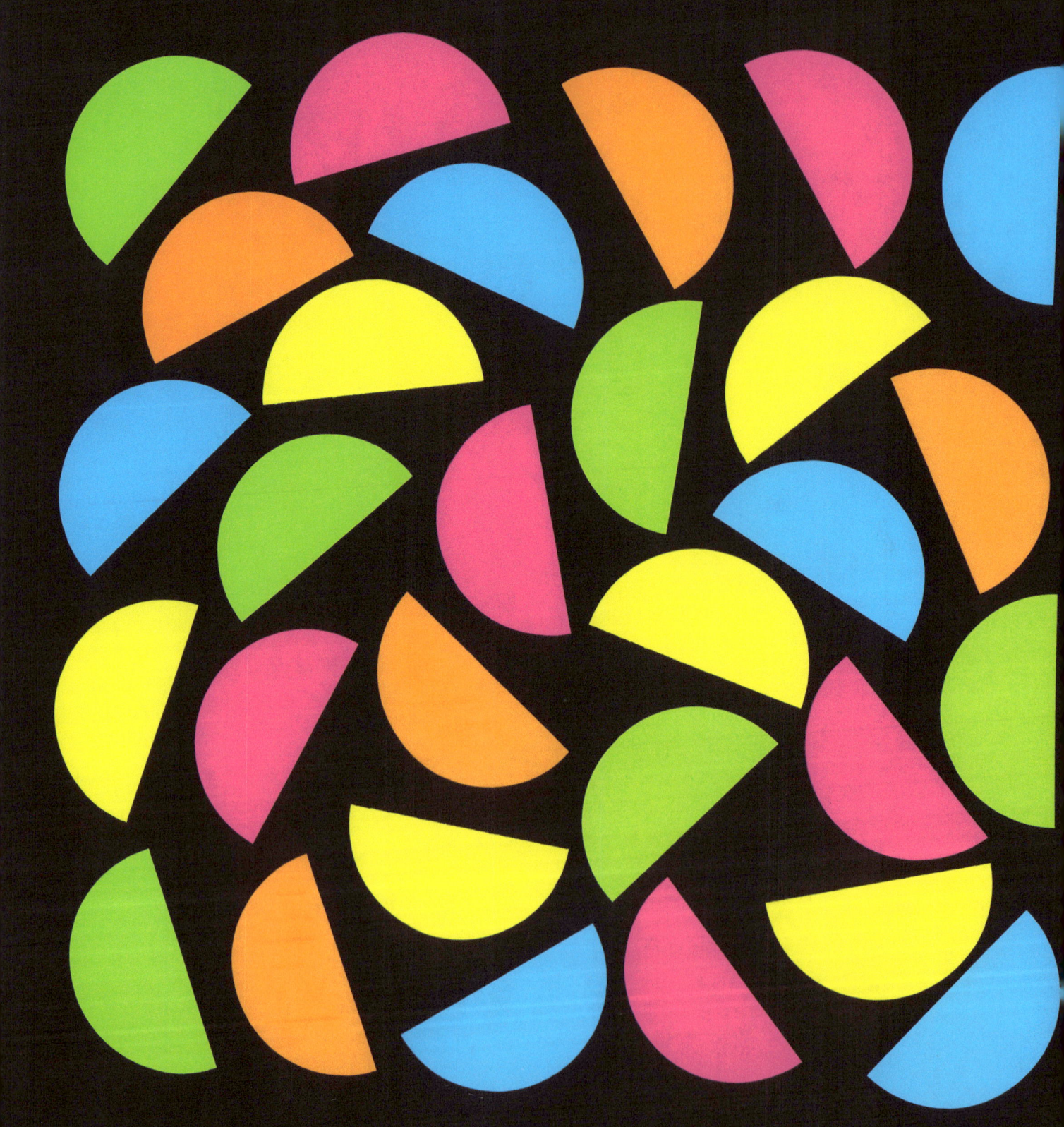

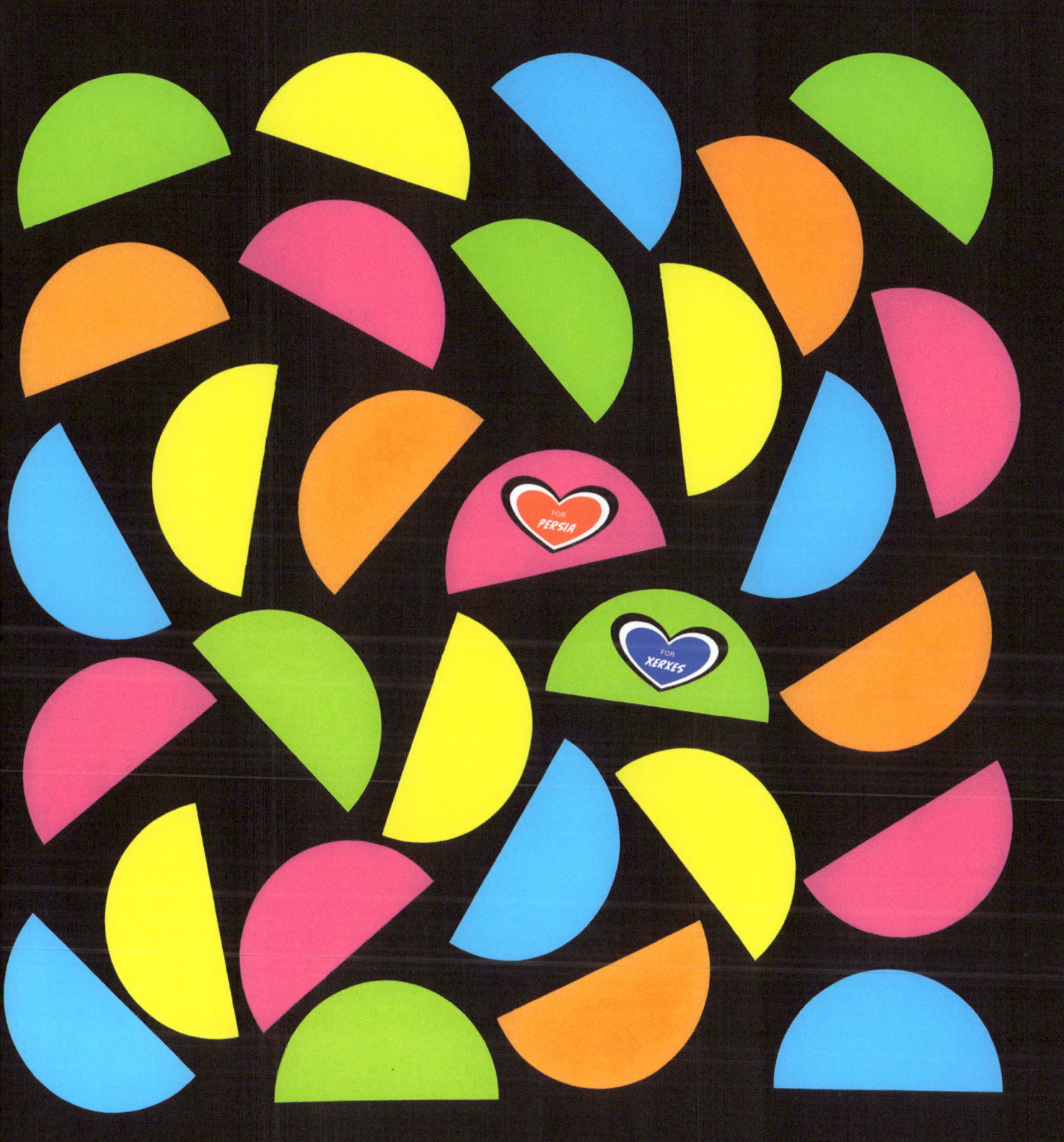

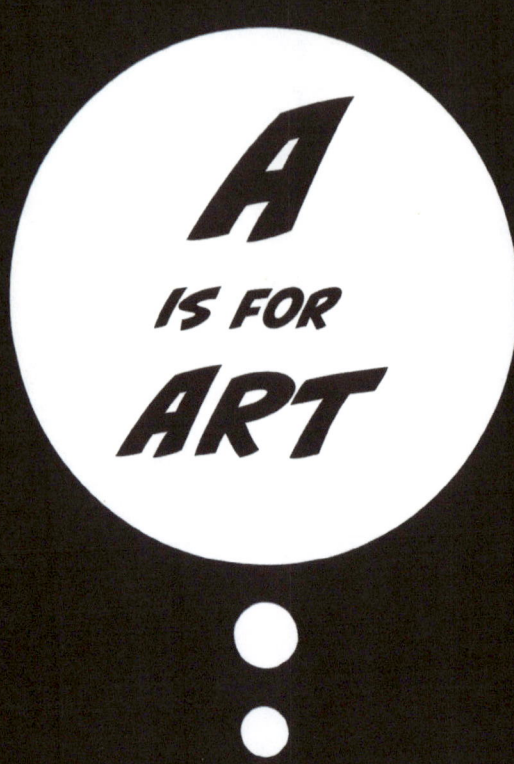

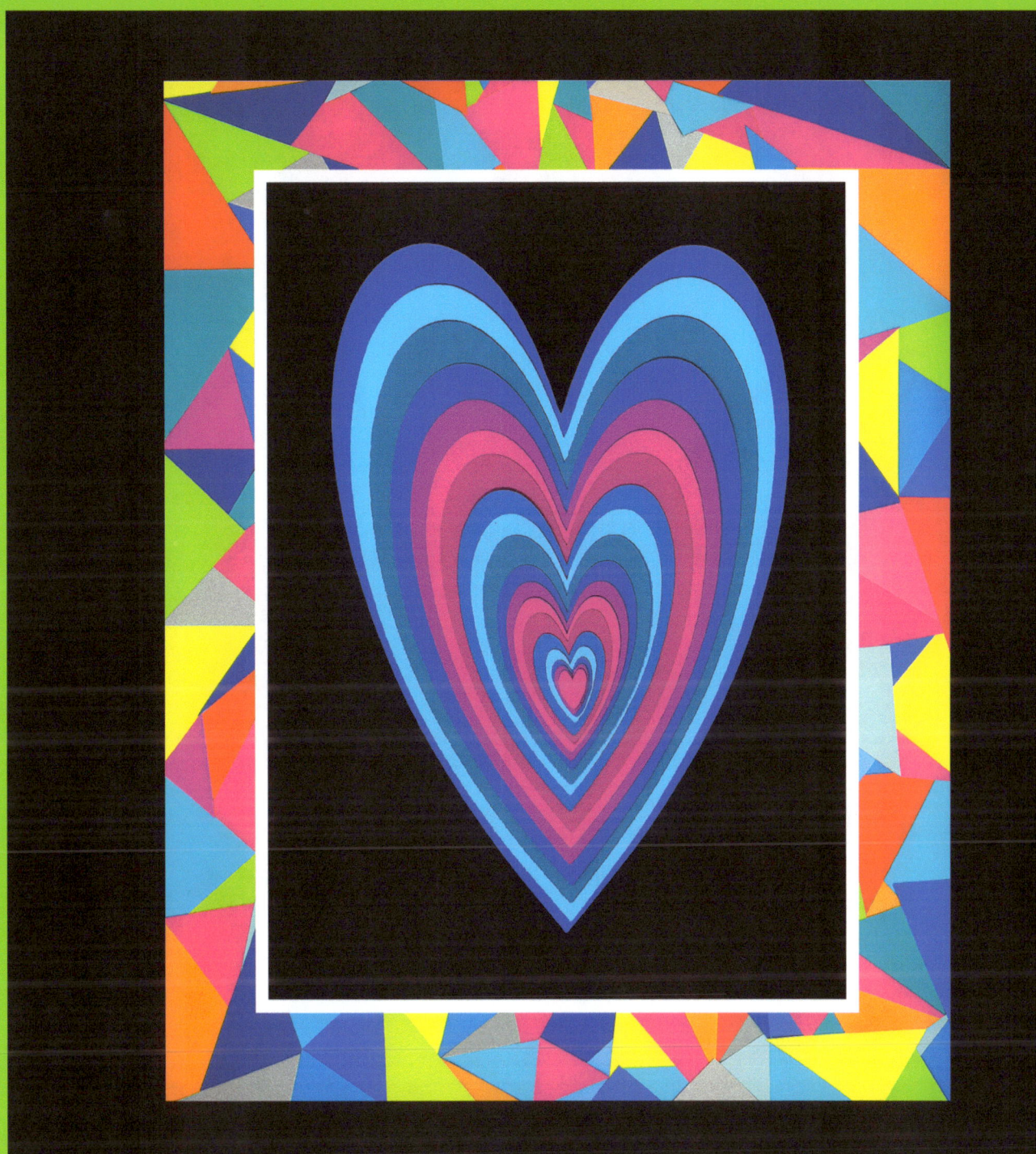

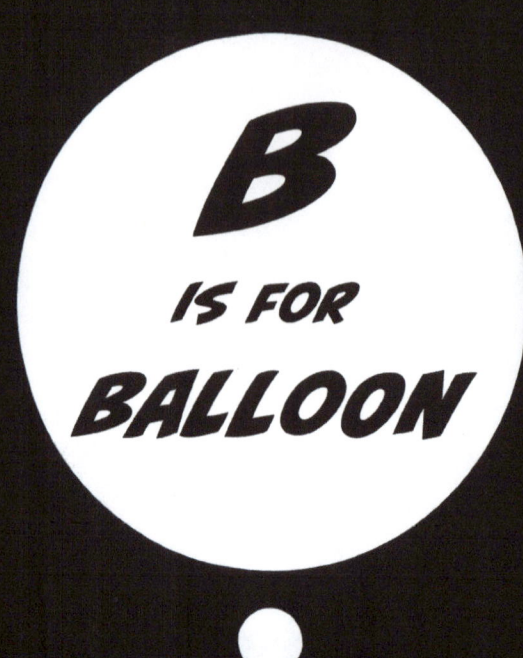

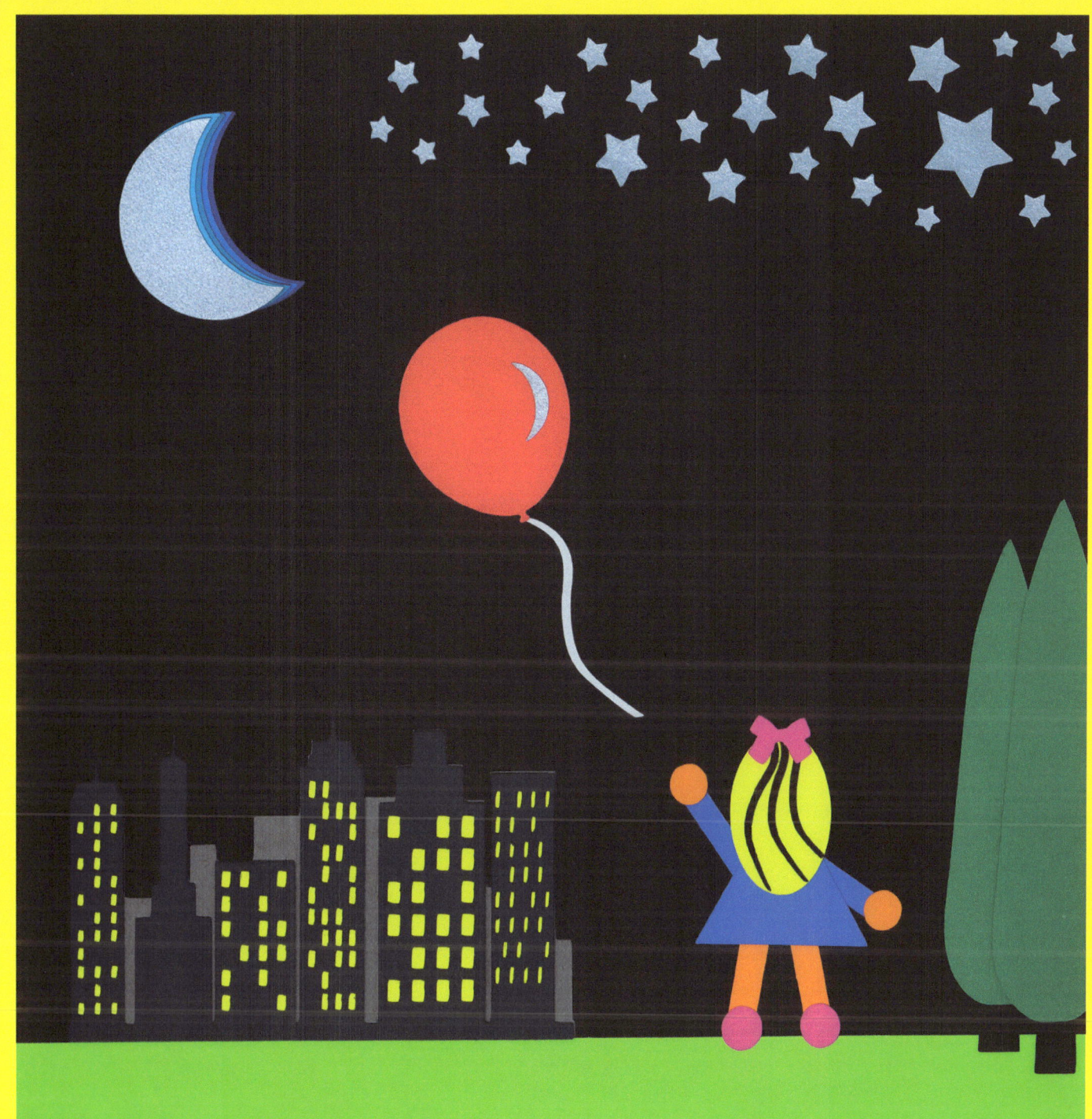

C IS FOR CAKE

...

WHICH YOU BAKE!

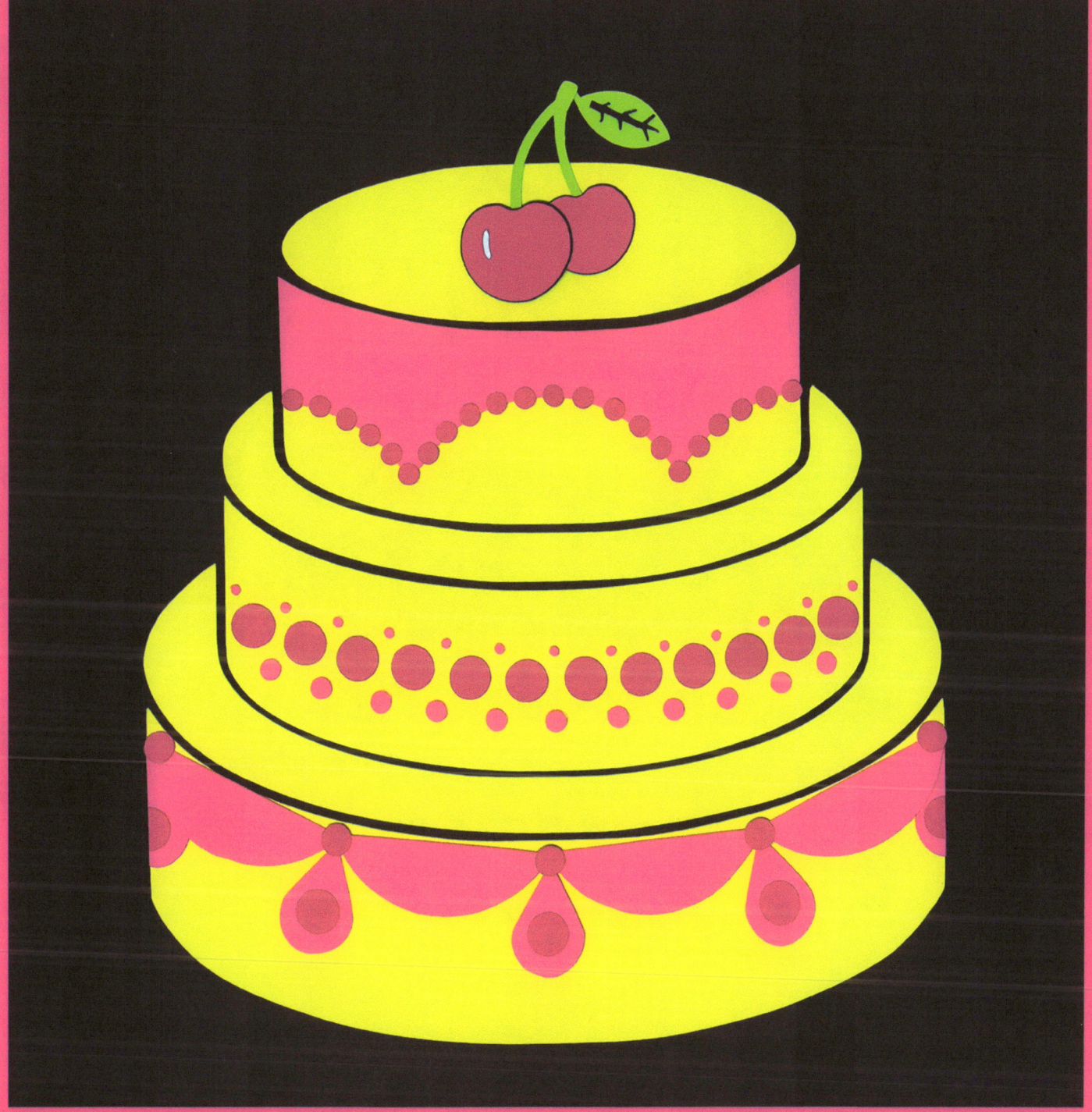

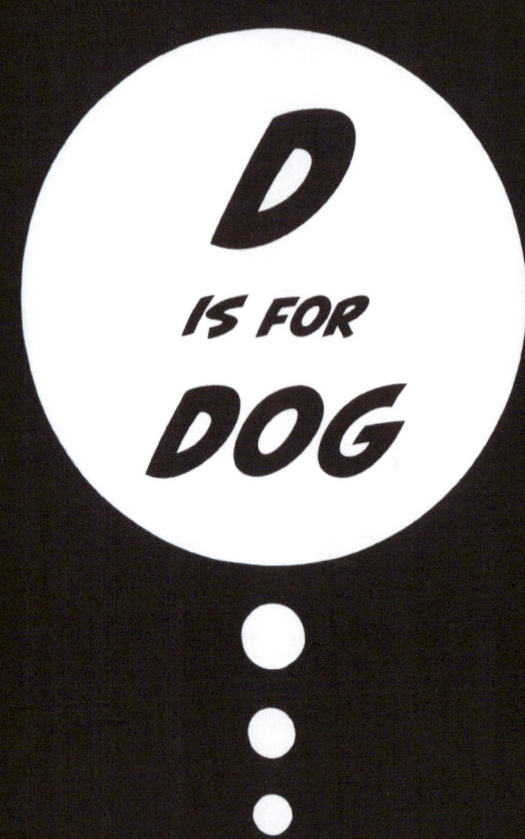

D
IS FOR
DOG

THIS DOG LOVES TO JOG!

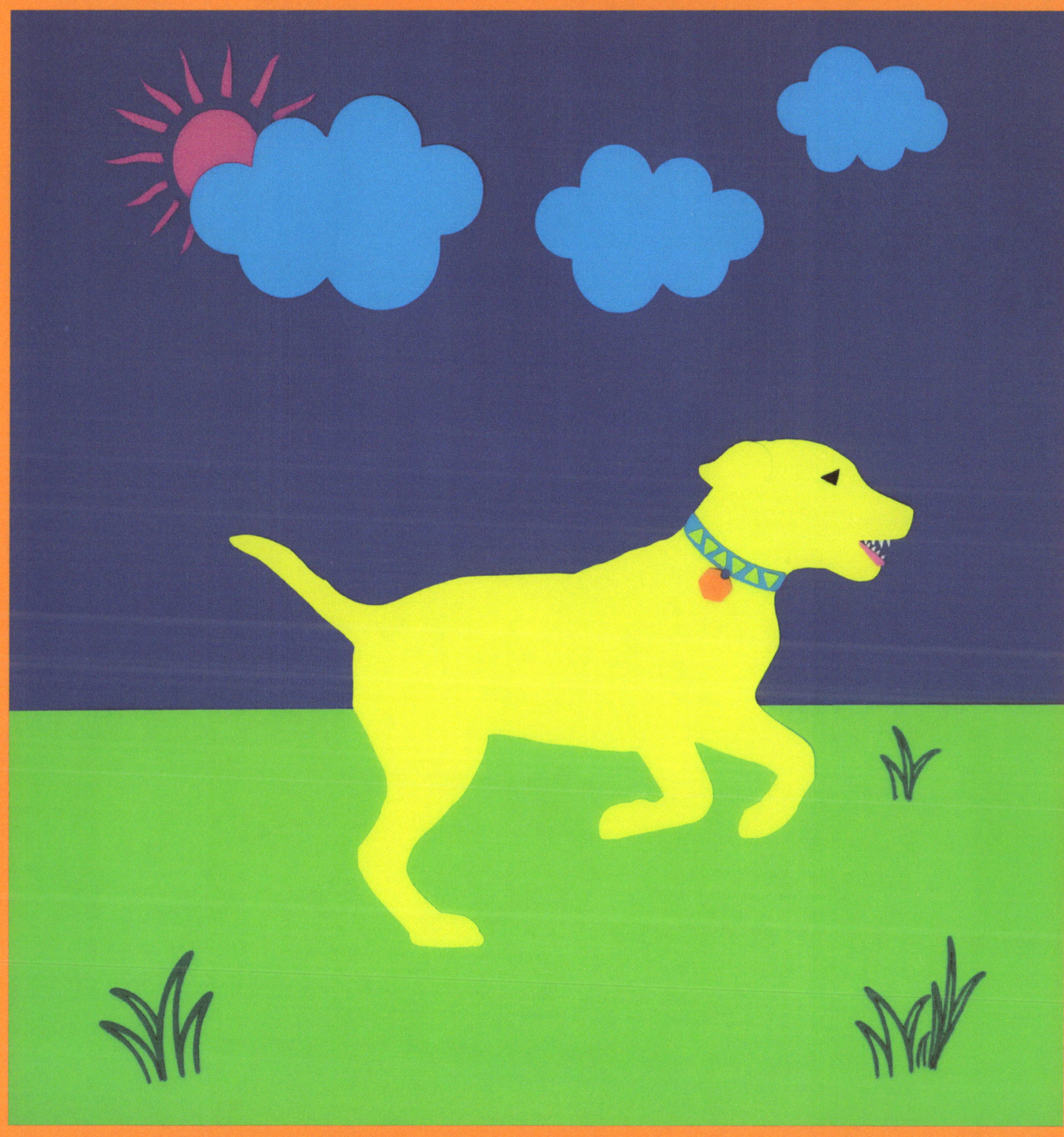

E
IS FOR
EAGLE

THIS EAGLE LOOKS REGAL!

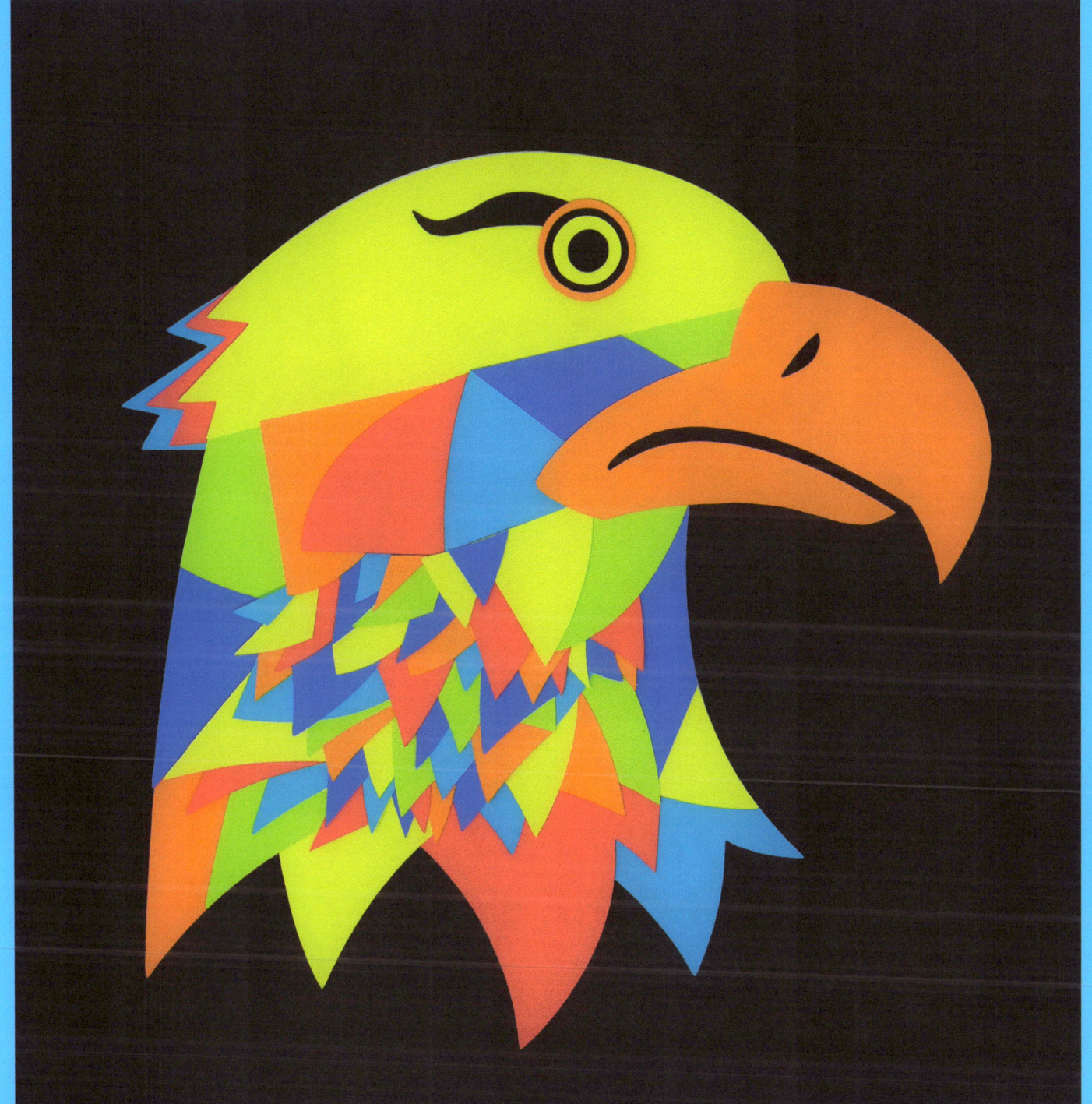

F

IS FOR

FOX

...

THIS FOX IS WEARING SOCKS!

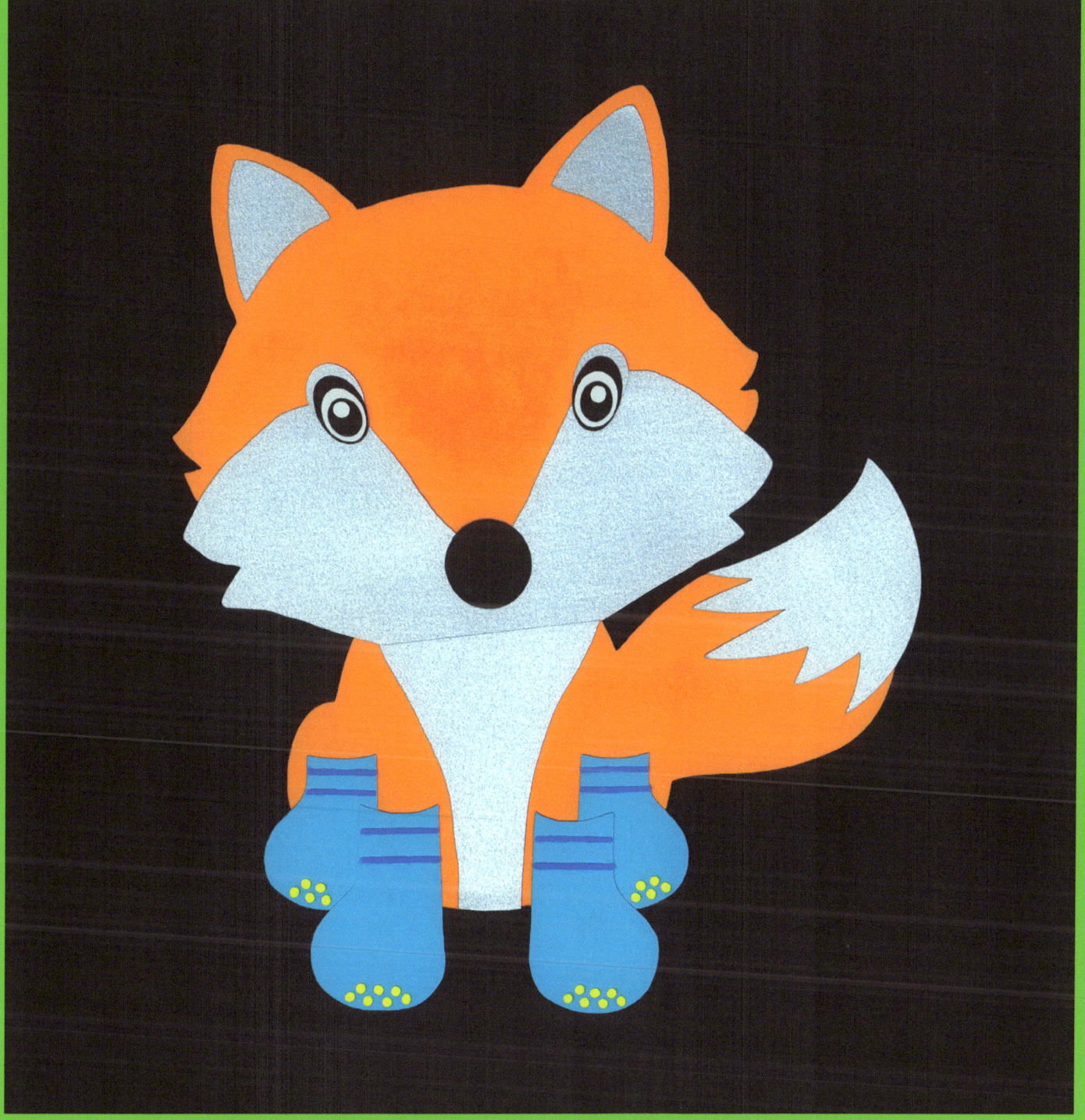

G IS FOR GOAT

THIS GOAT IS ON A BOAT!

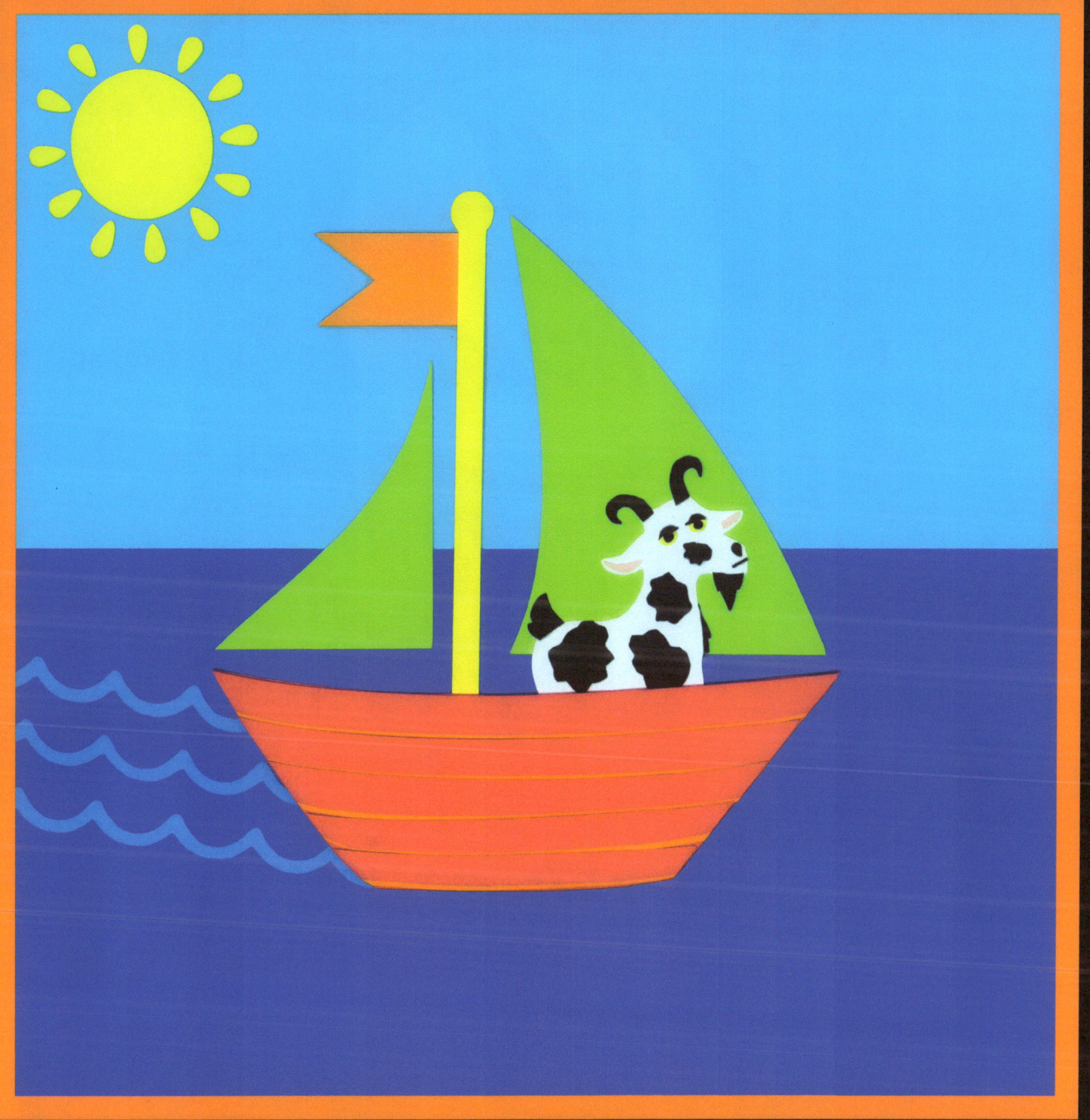

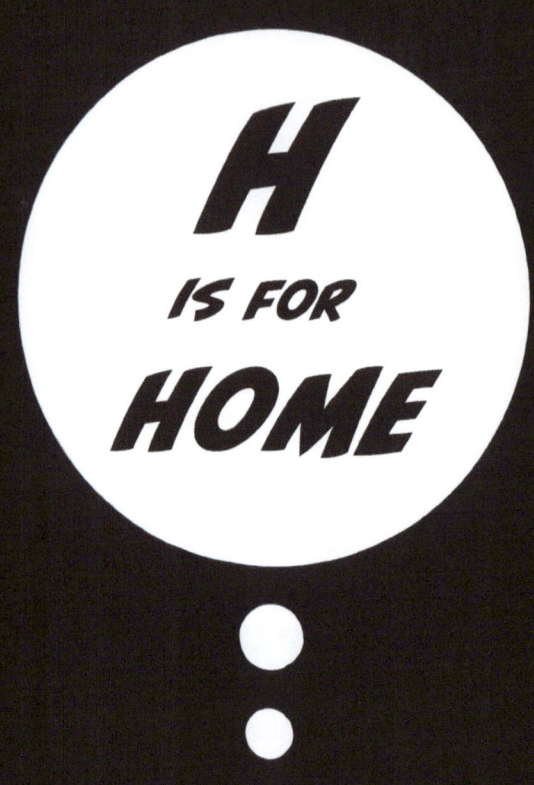

H
IS FOR
HOME

THERE IS A GNOME AT THIS HOME!

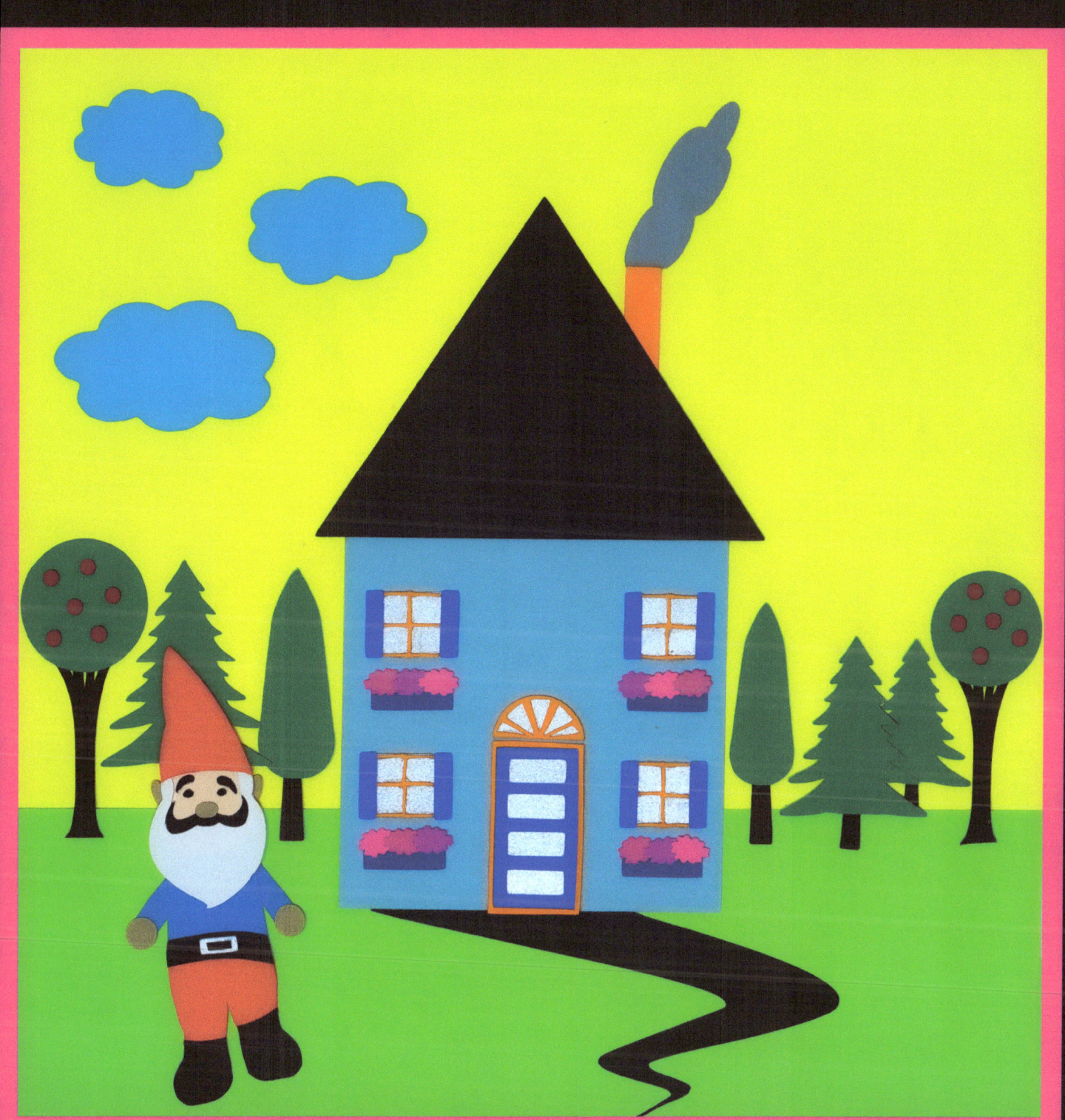

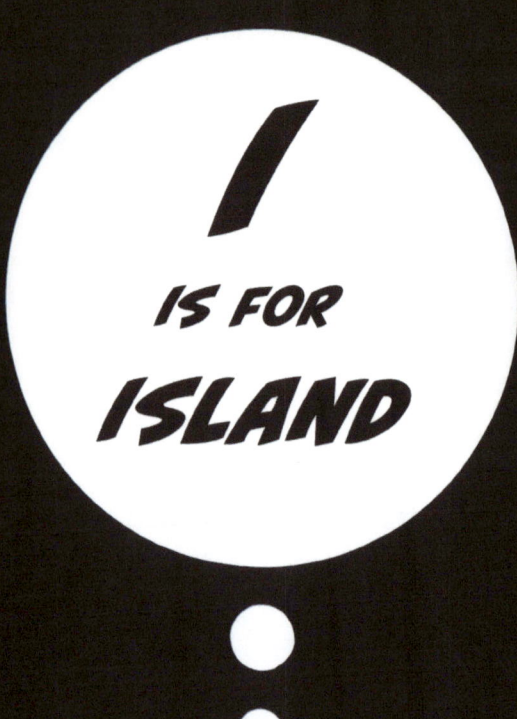

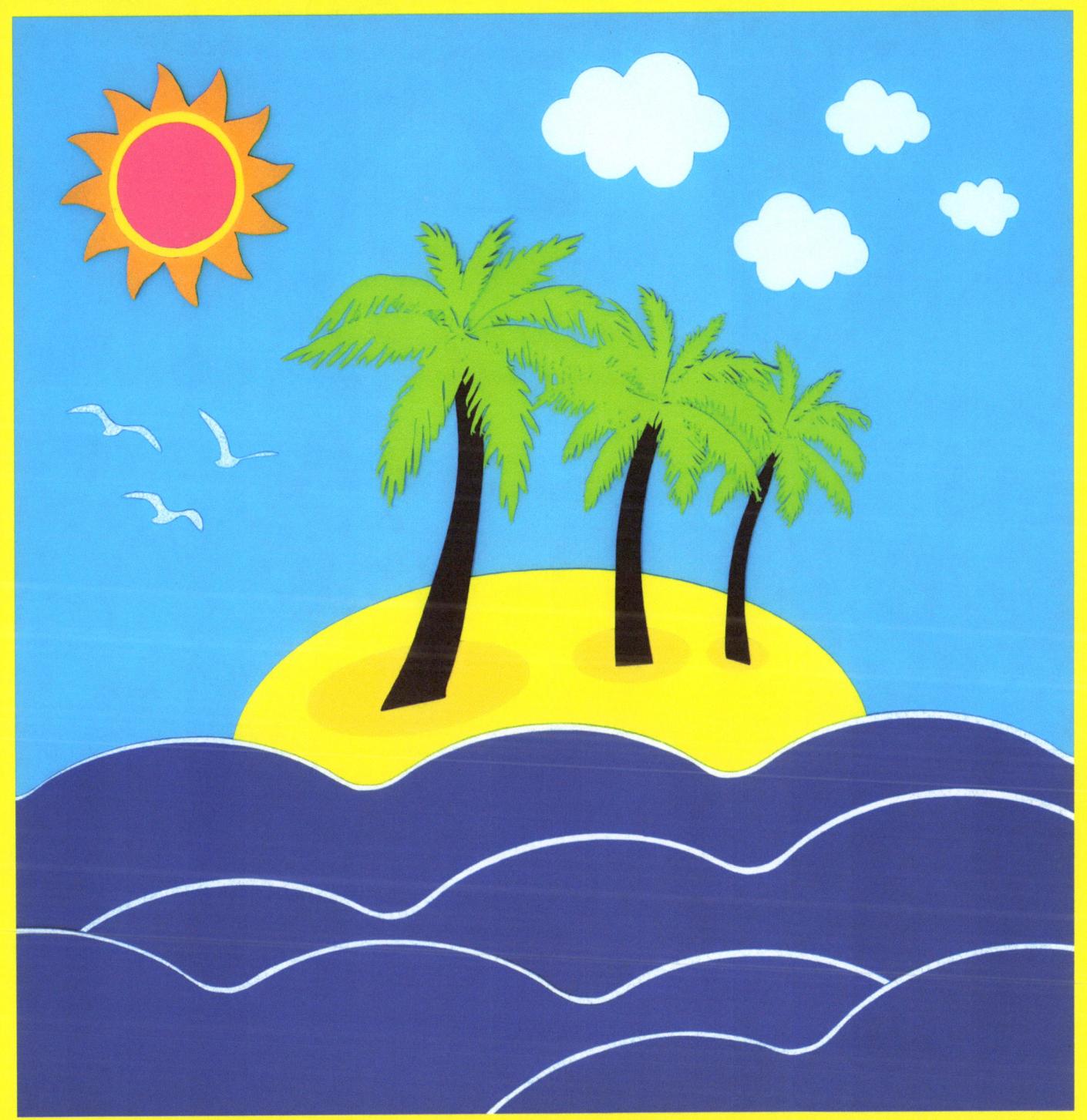

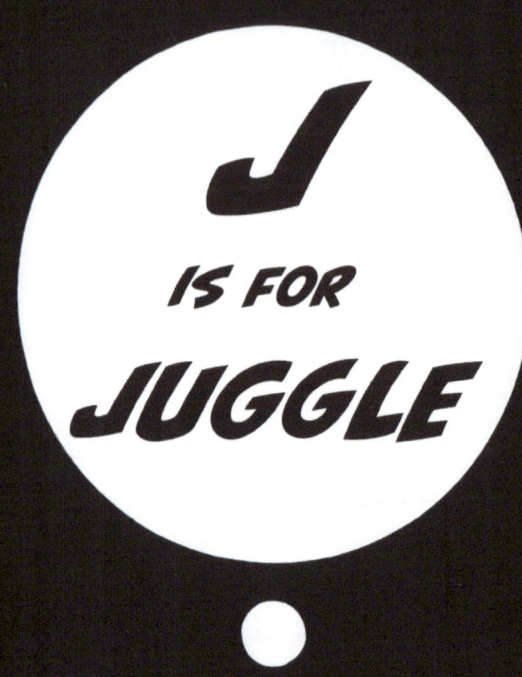

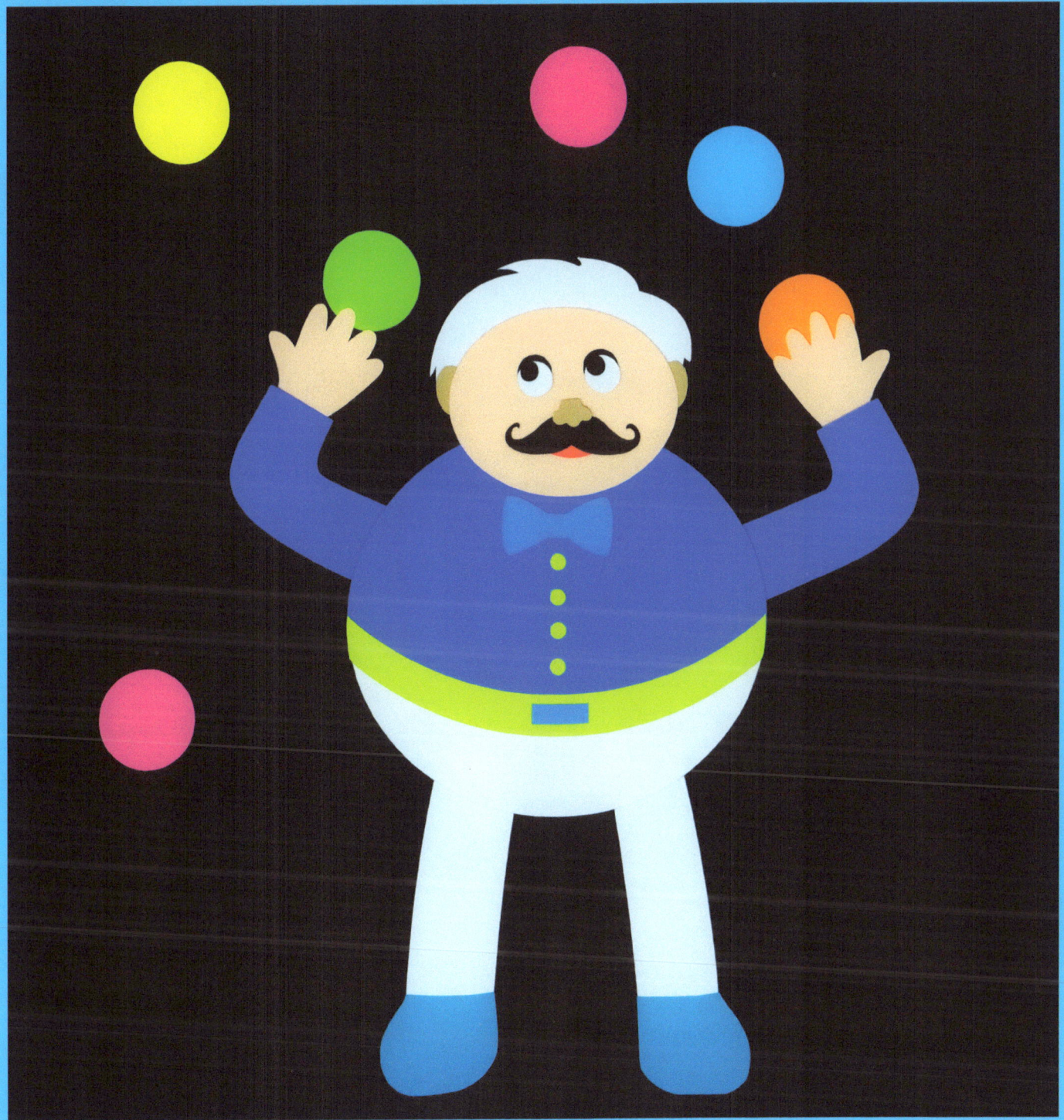

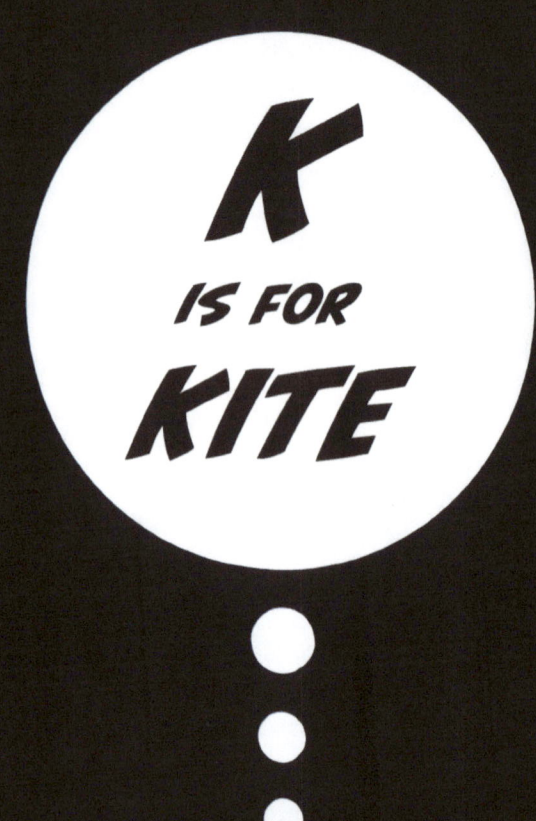

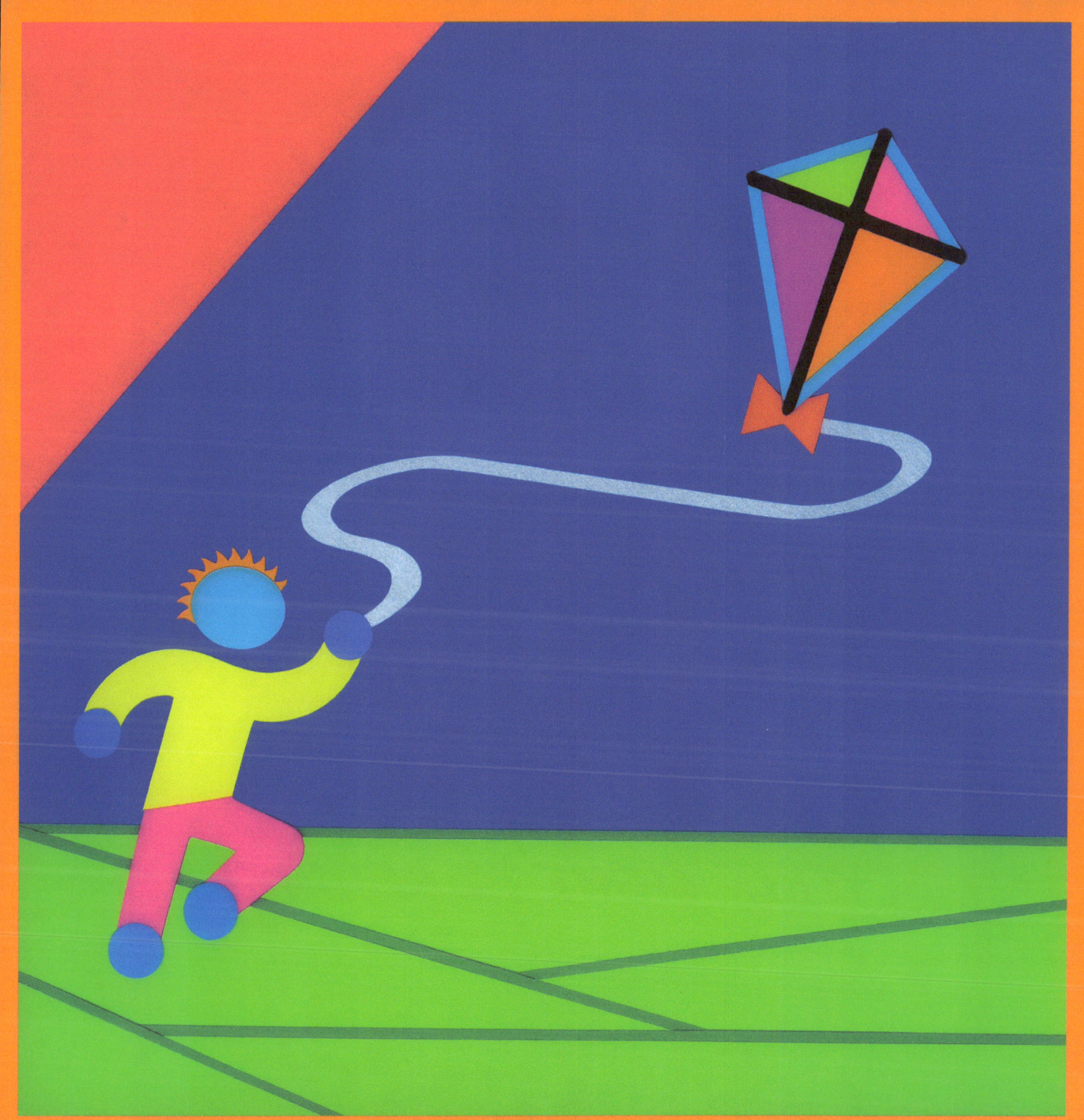

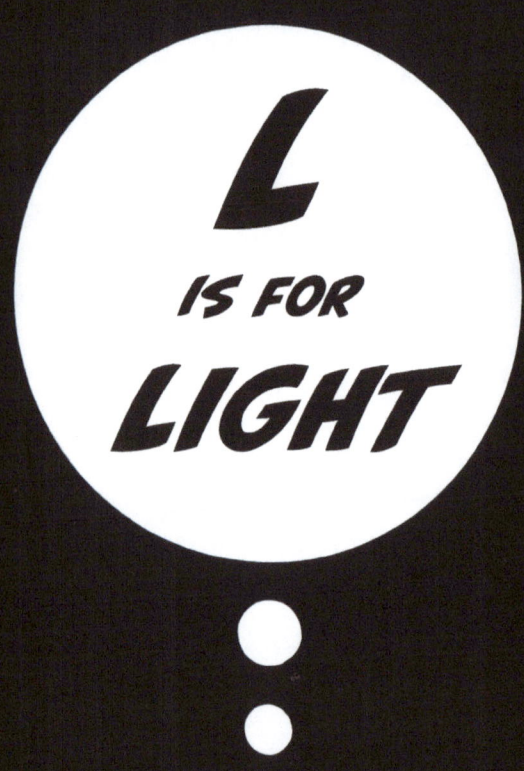

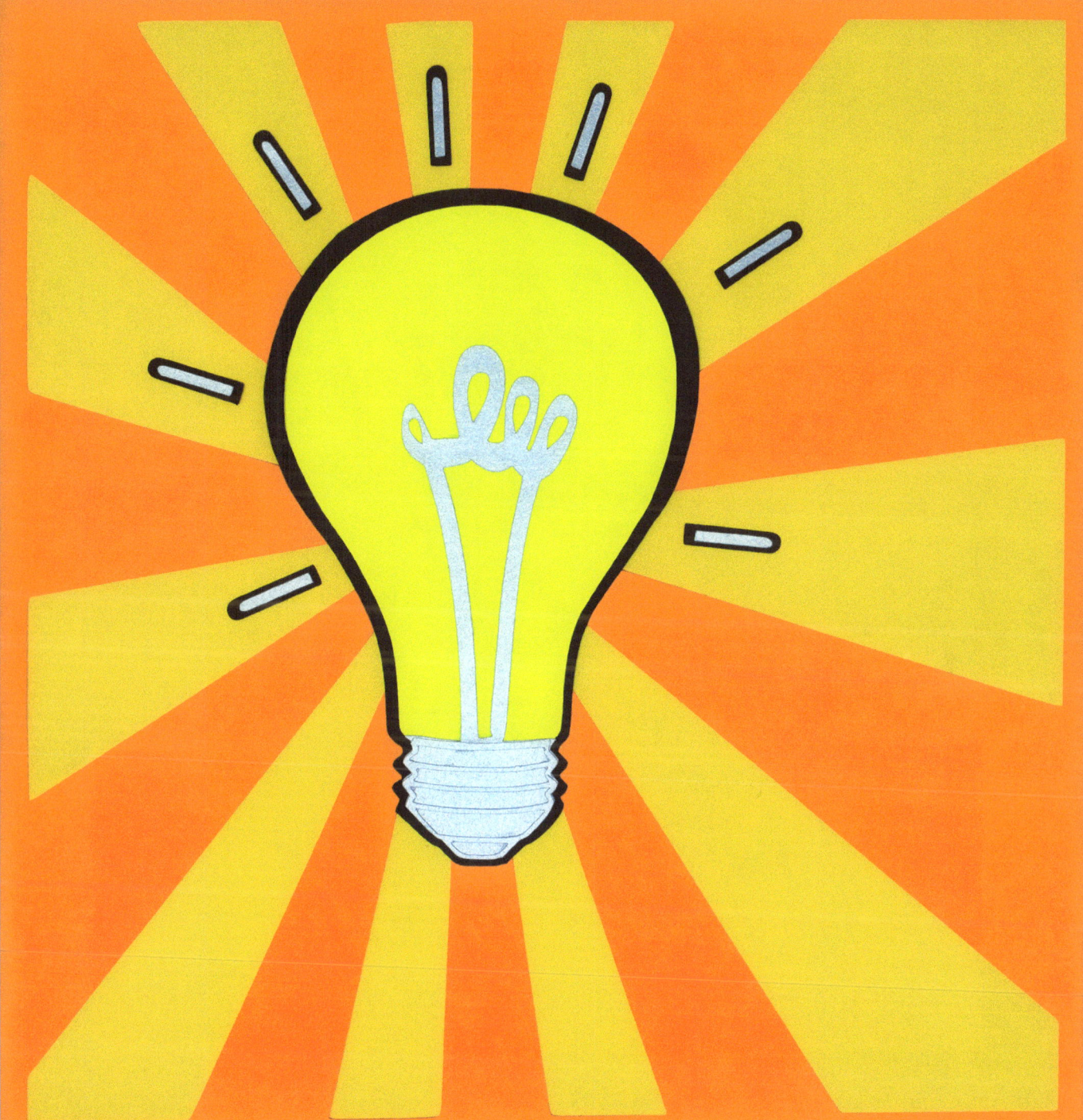

M
IS FOR
MONKEY

THIS MONKEY IS A BANANA JUNKIE!

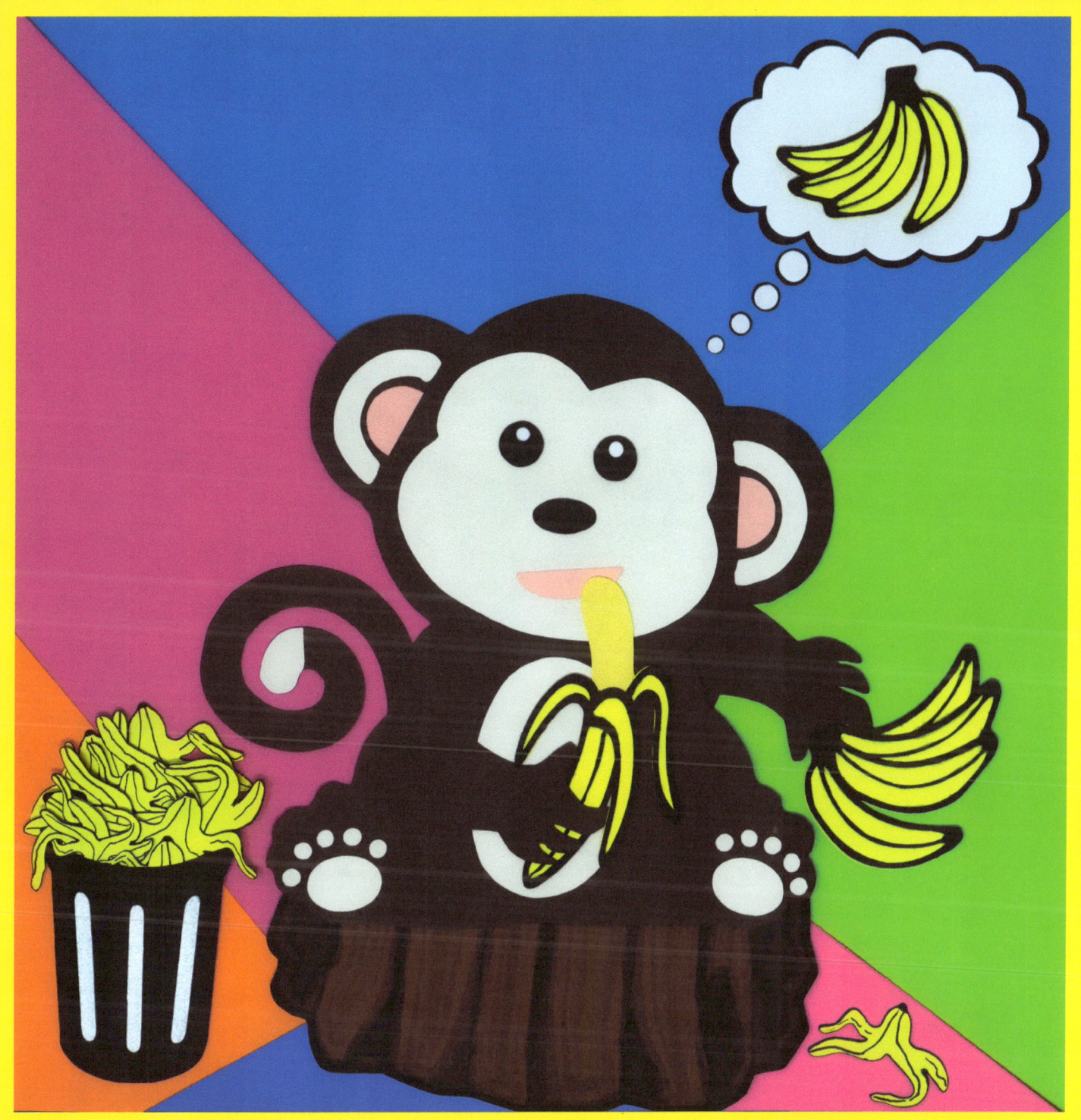

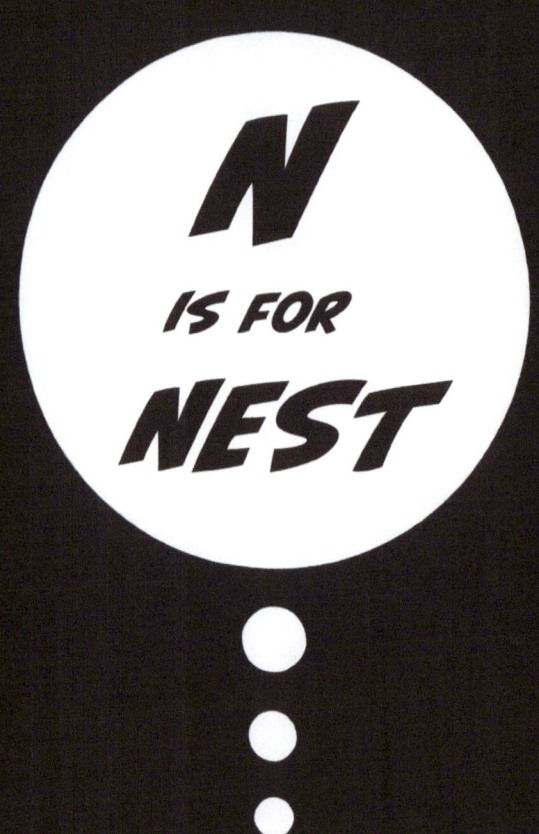

N
IS FOR
NEST

WHERE BIRDS REST!

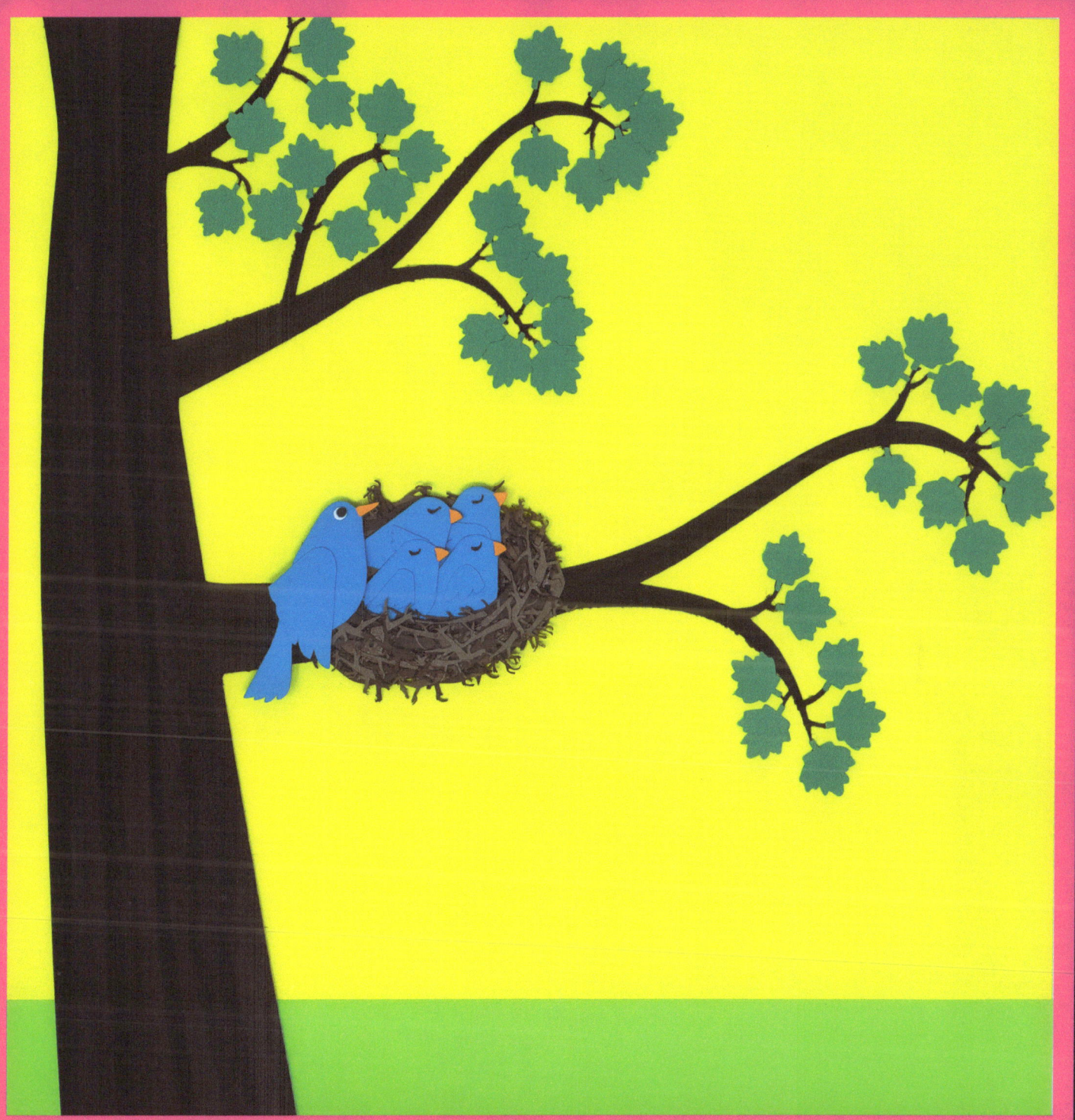

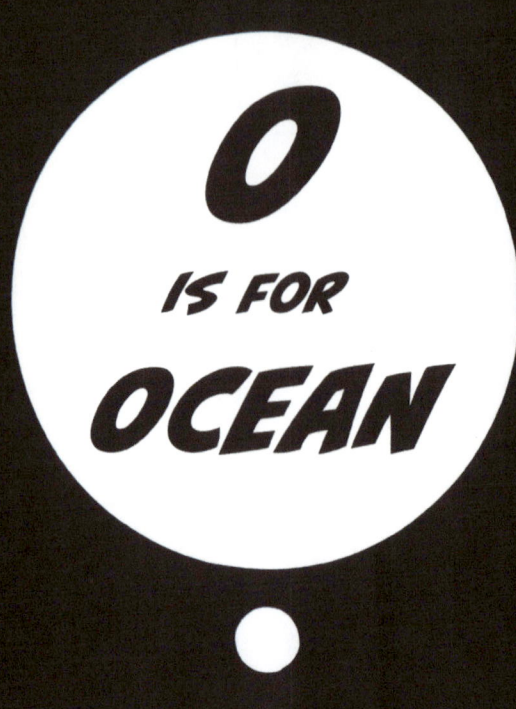

O IS FOR OCEAN

THE OCEAN HAS CONSTANT MOTION!

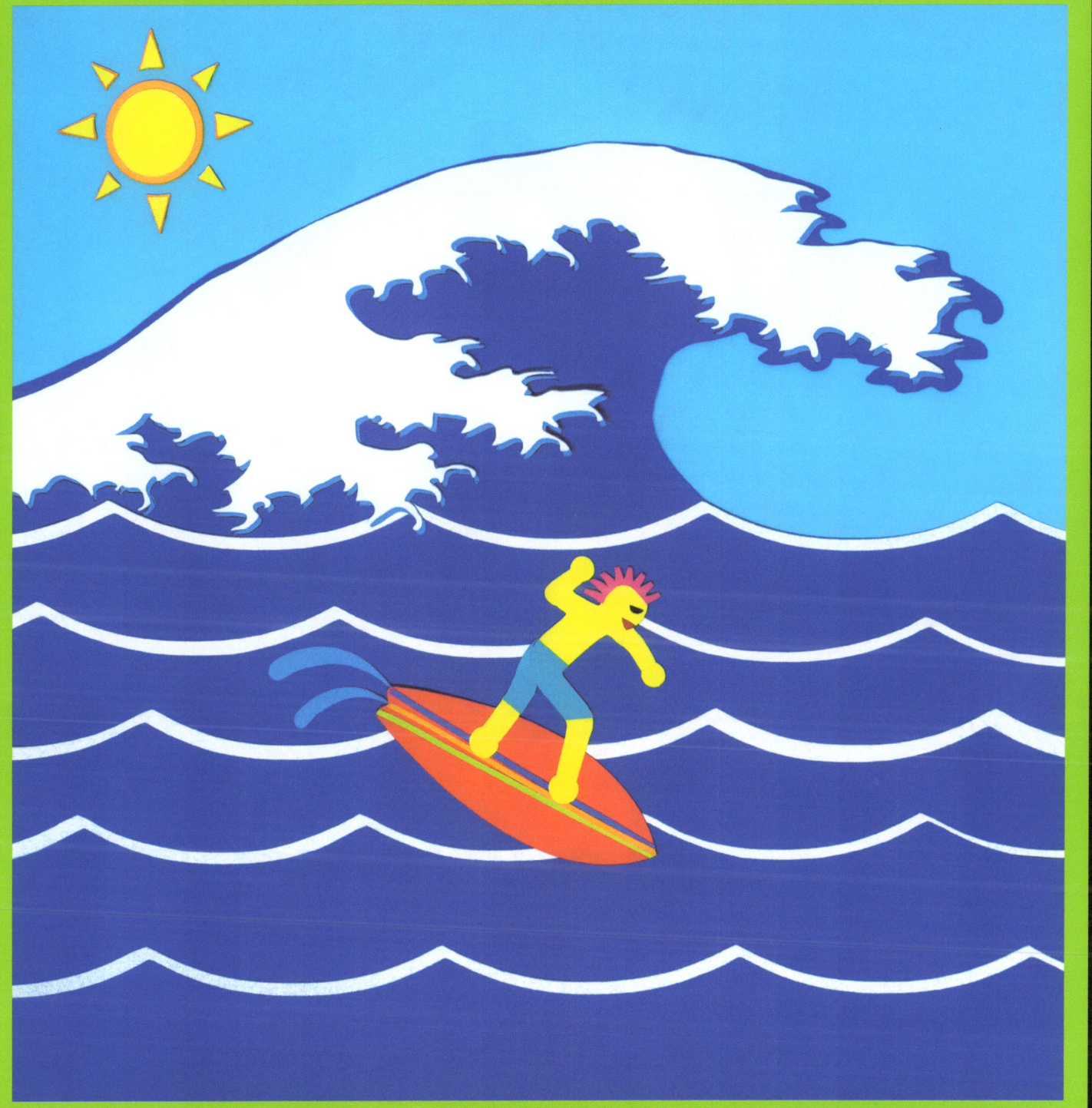

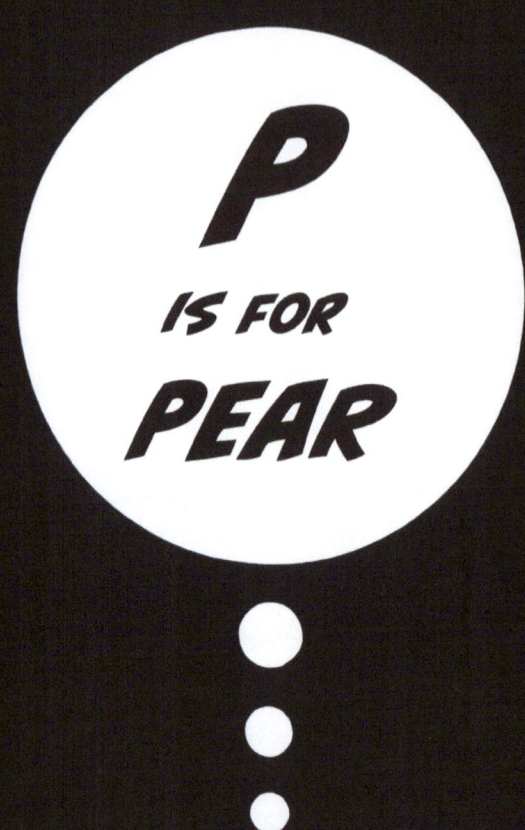

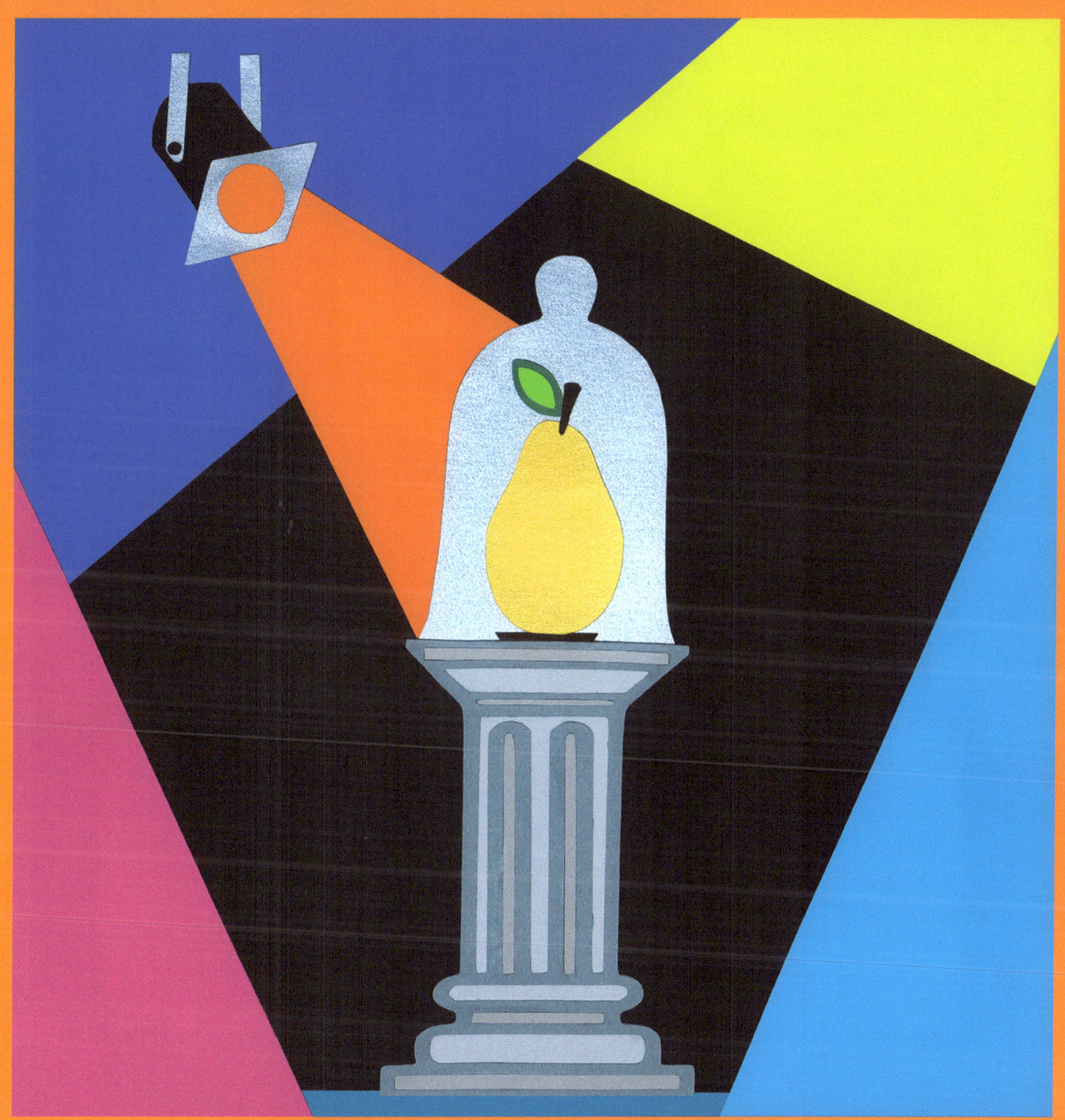

Q

IS FOR

QUEEN

. . .

THIS QUEEN IS WEARING GREEN!

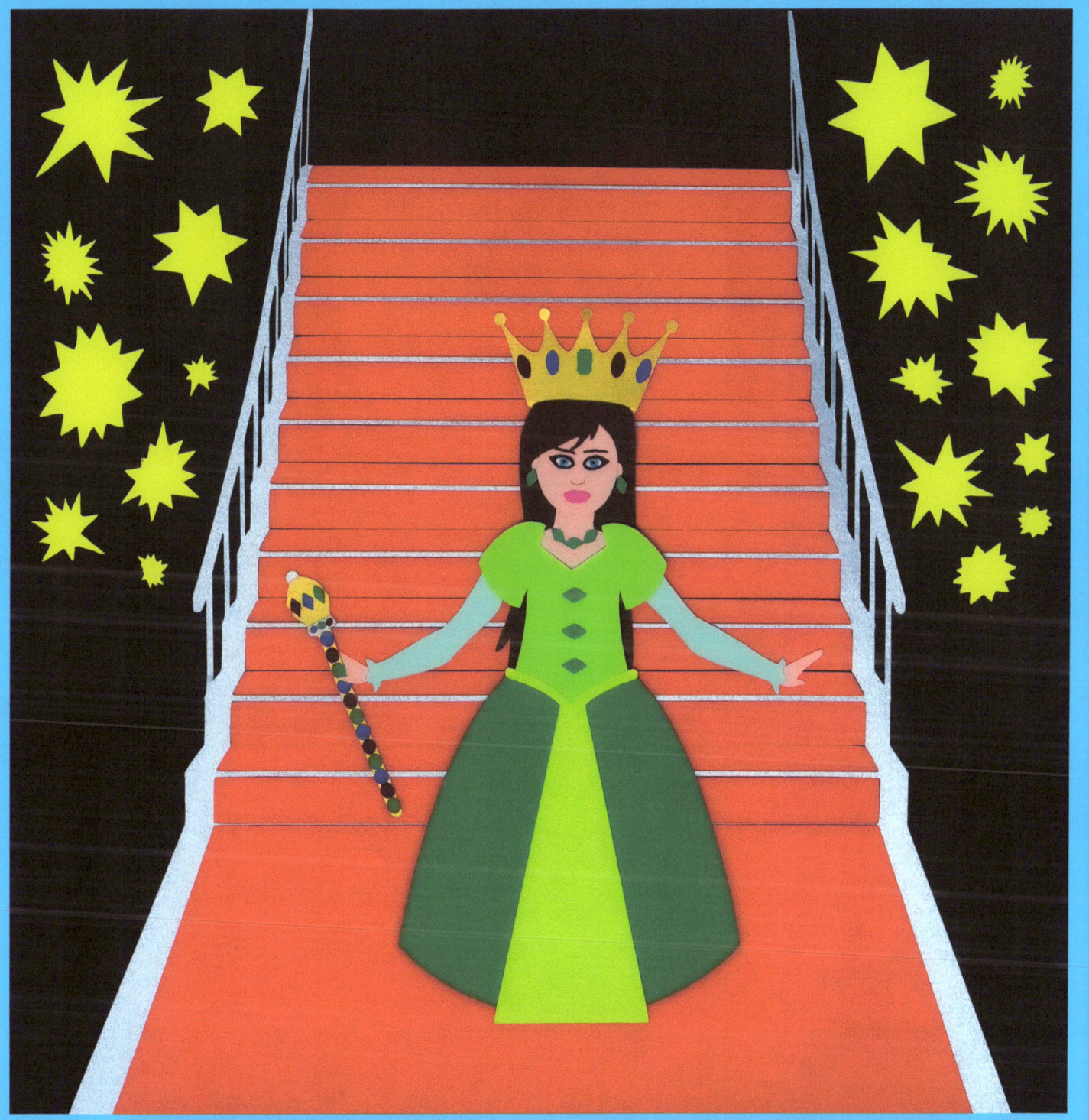

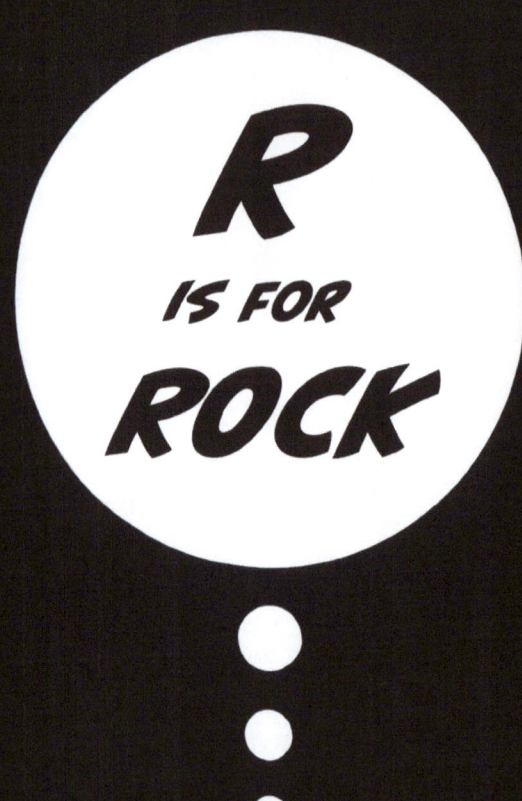

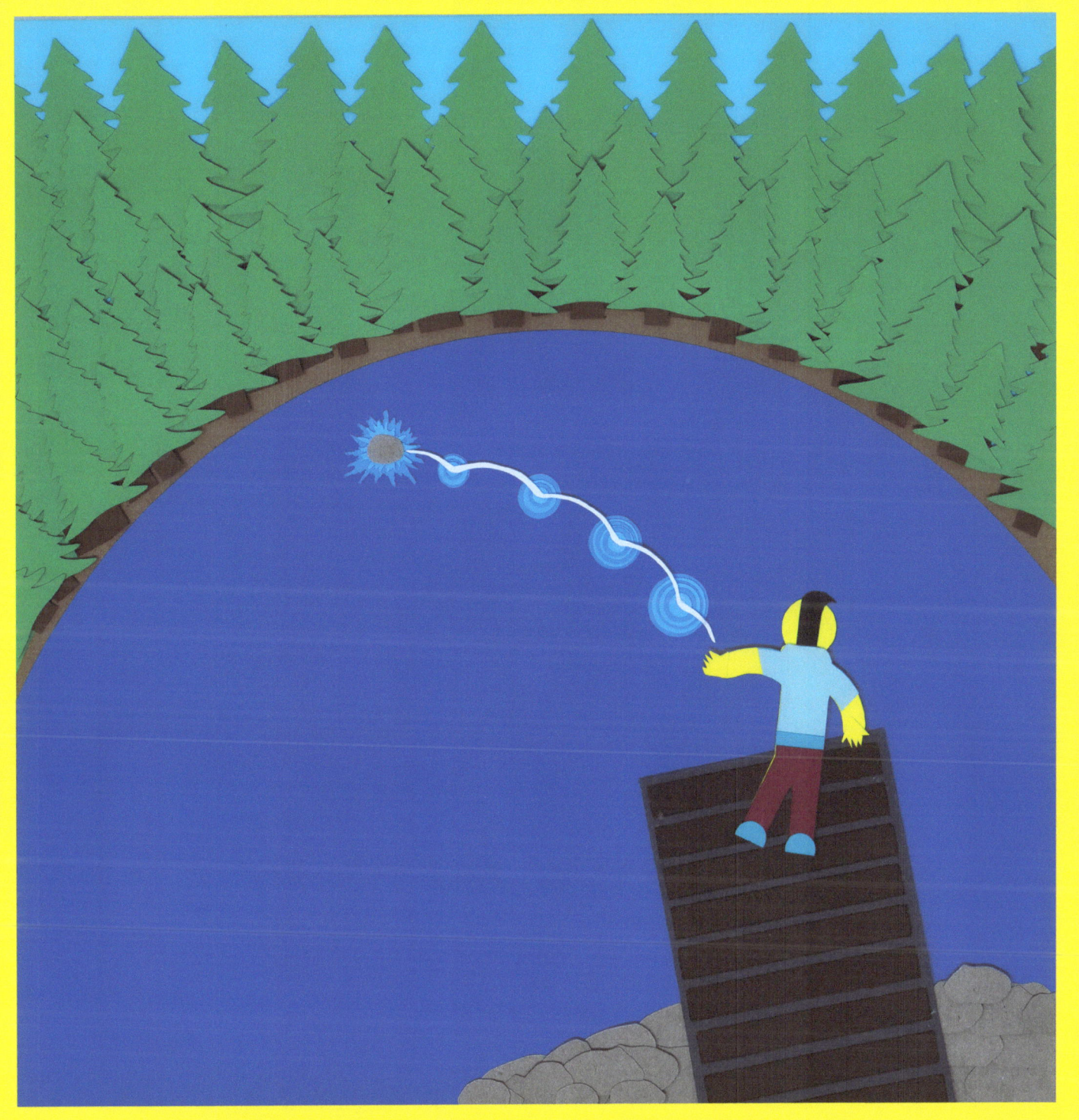

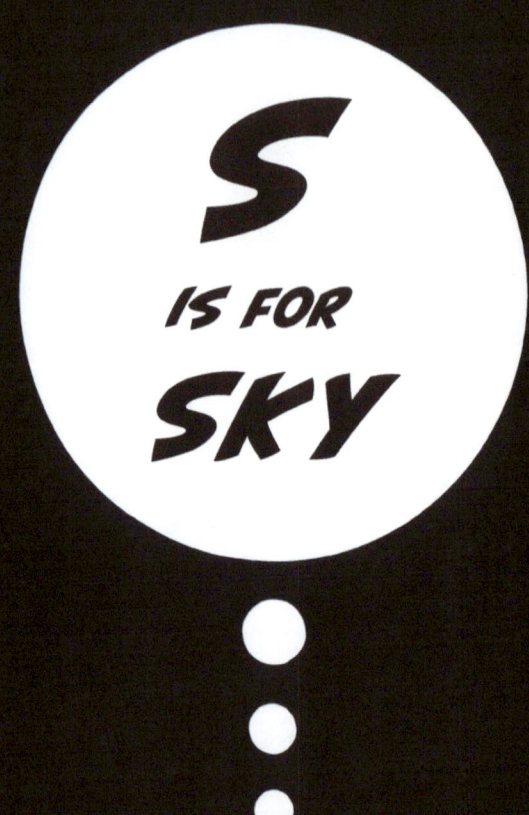

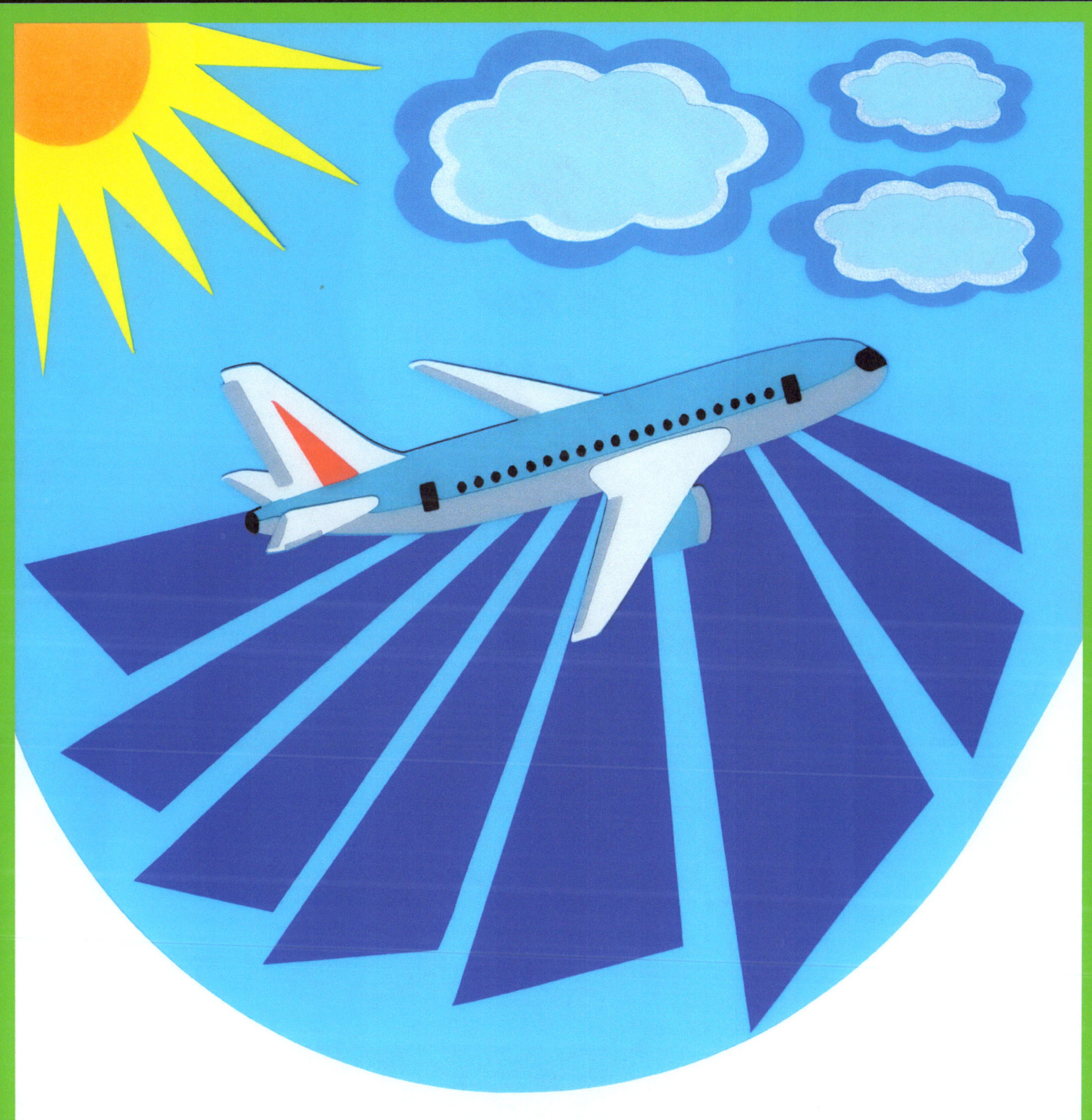

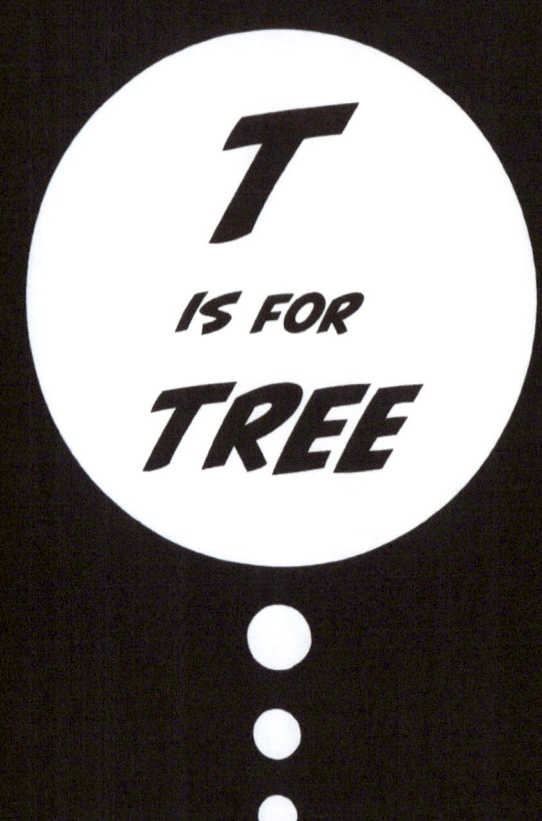

T IS FOR TREE

POLLINATED BY BEES!

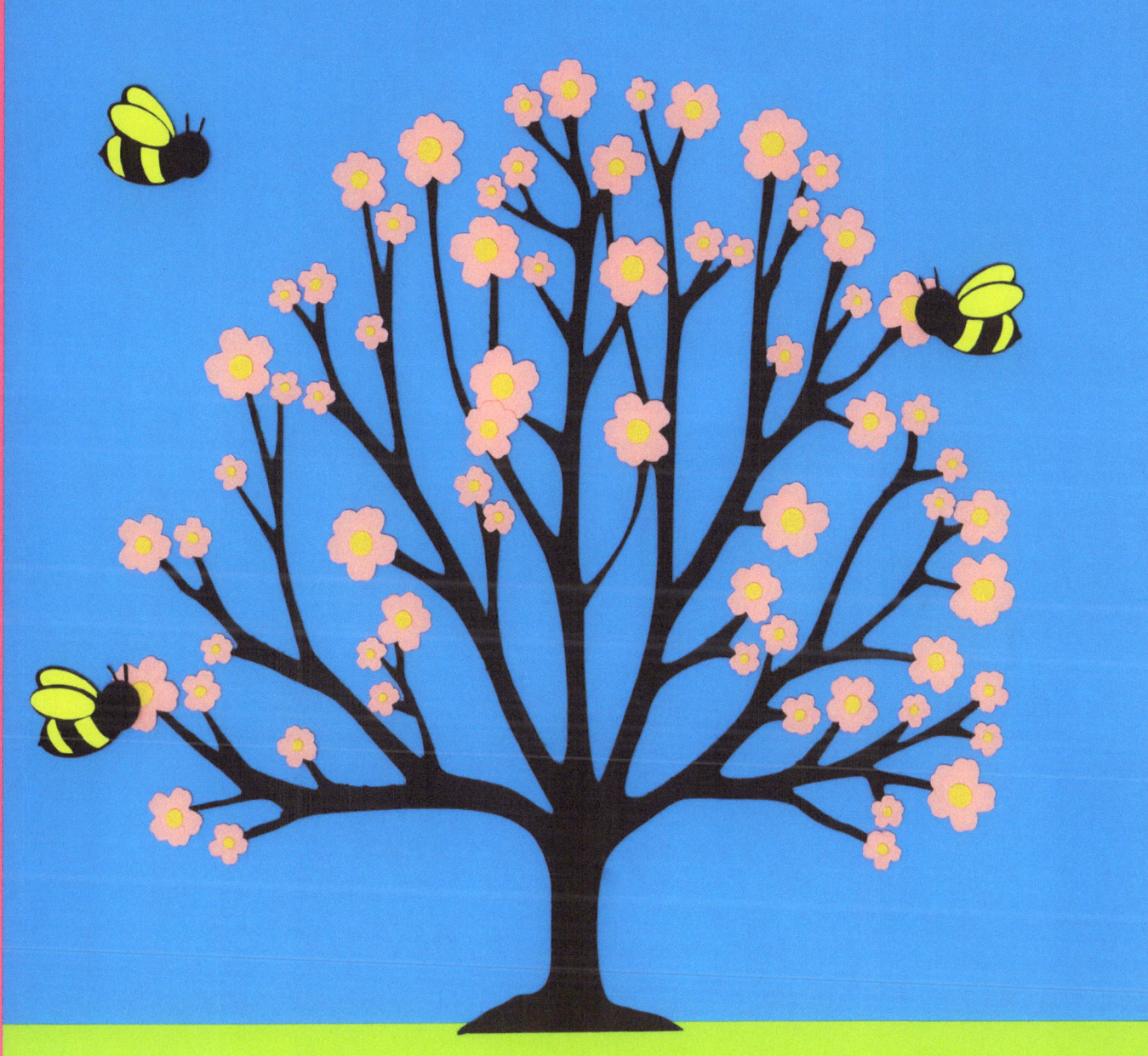

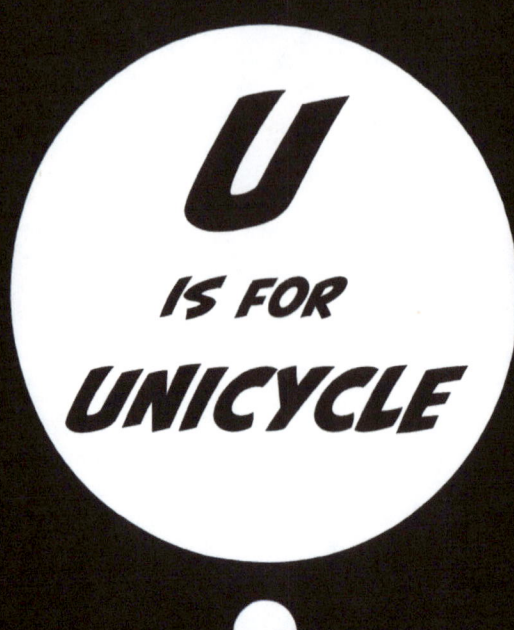

U
IS FOR
UNICYCLE

WHICH IS HALF OF A BICYCLE!

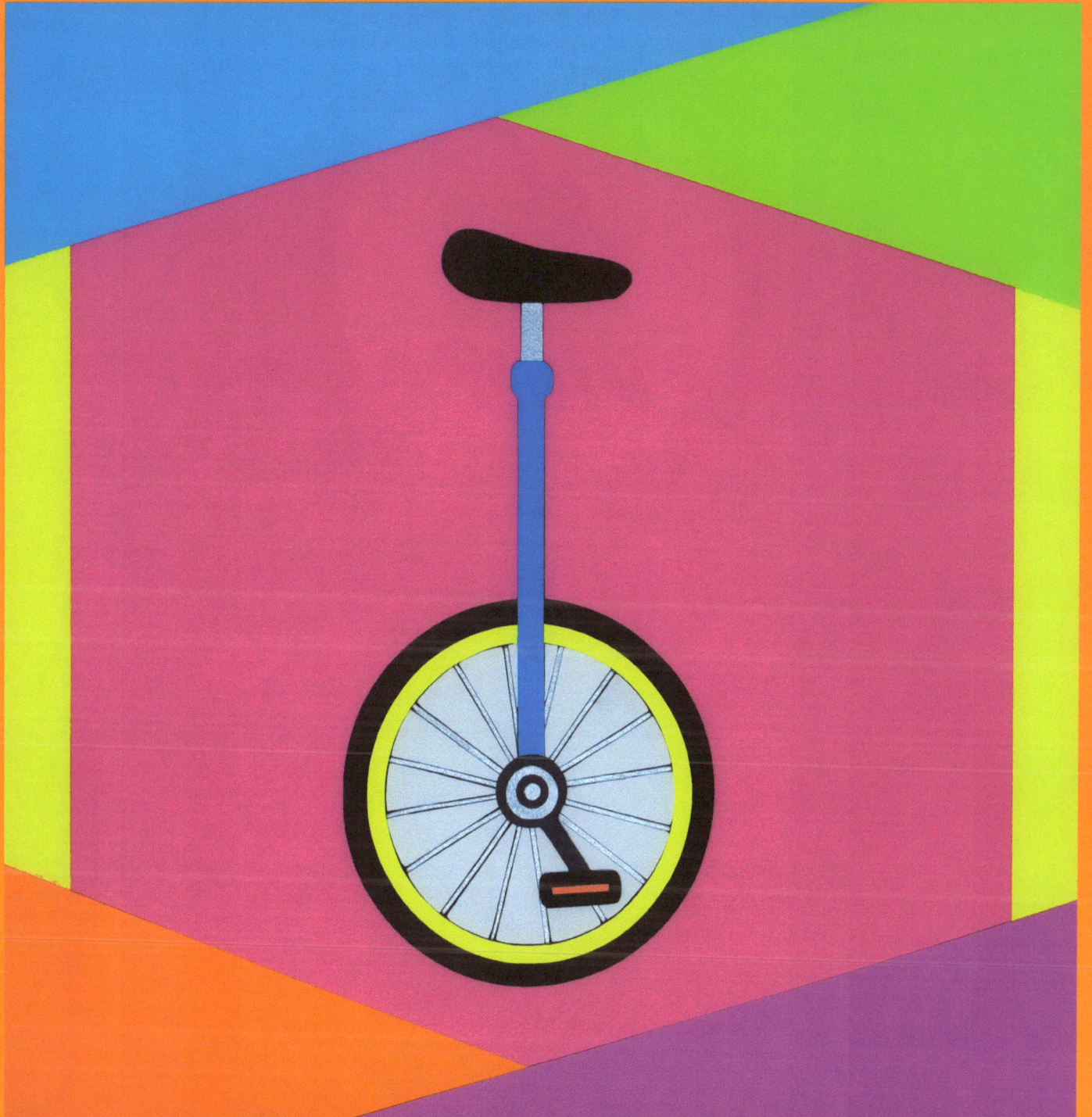

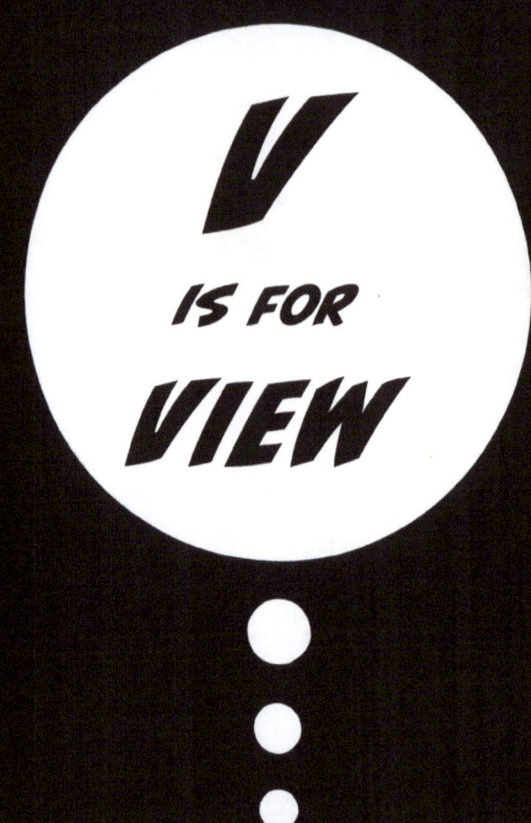

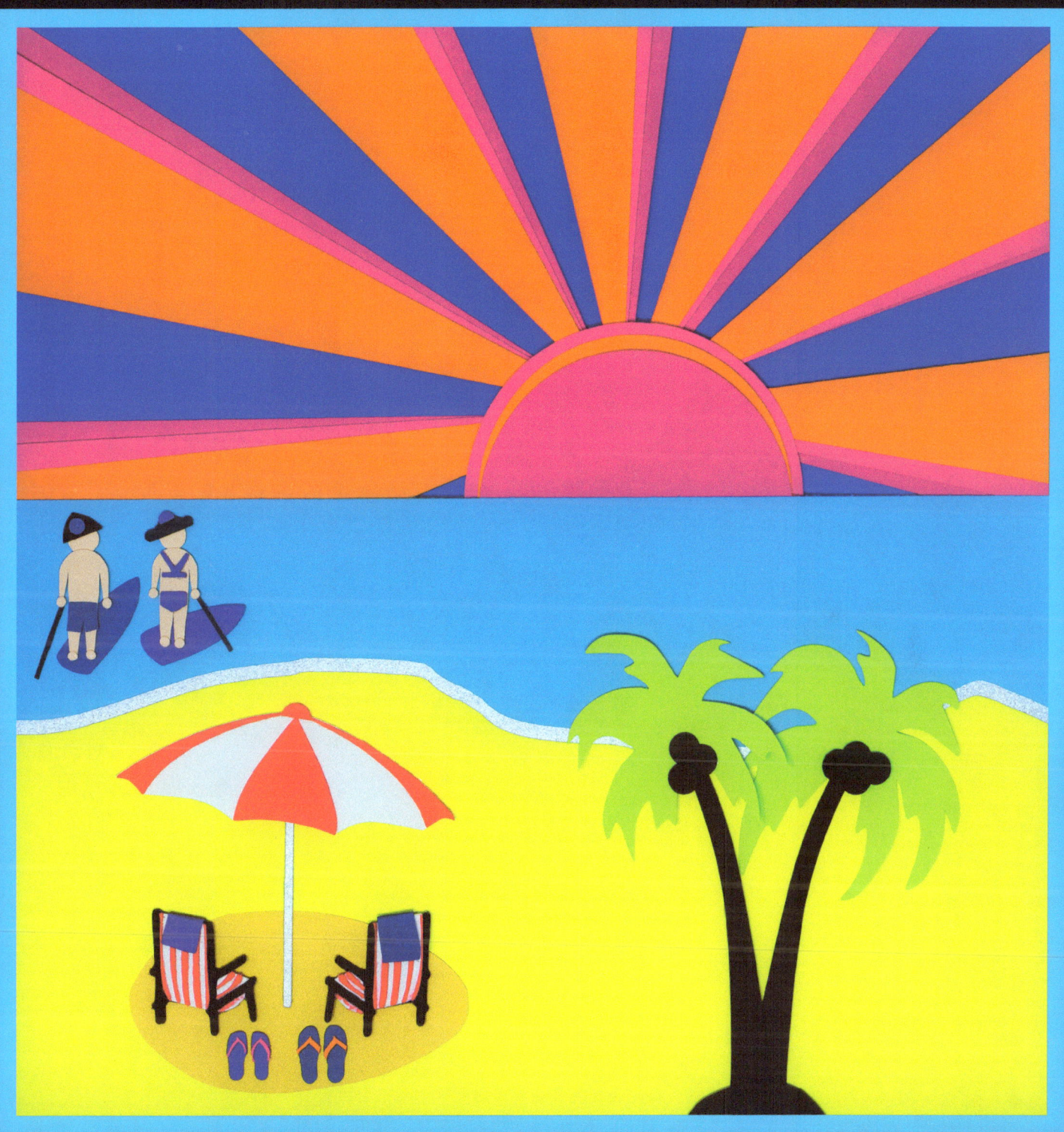

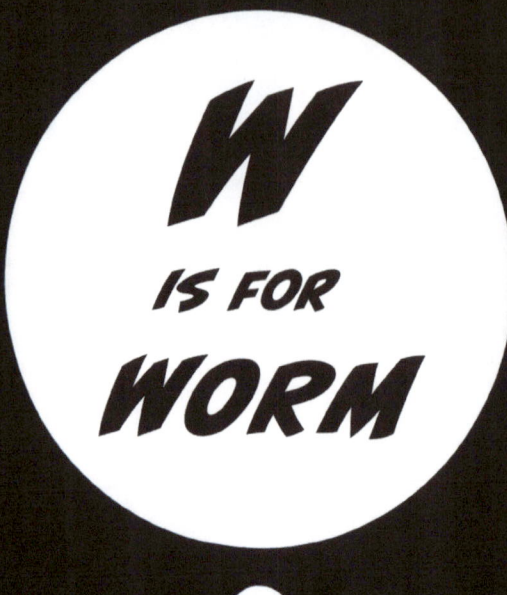

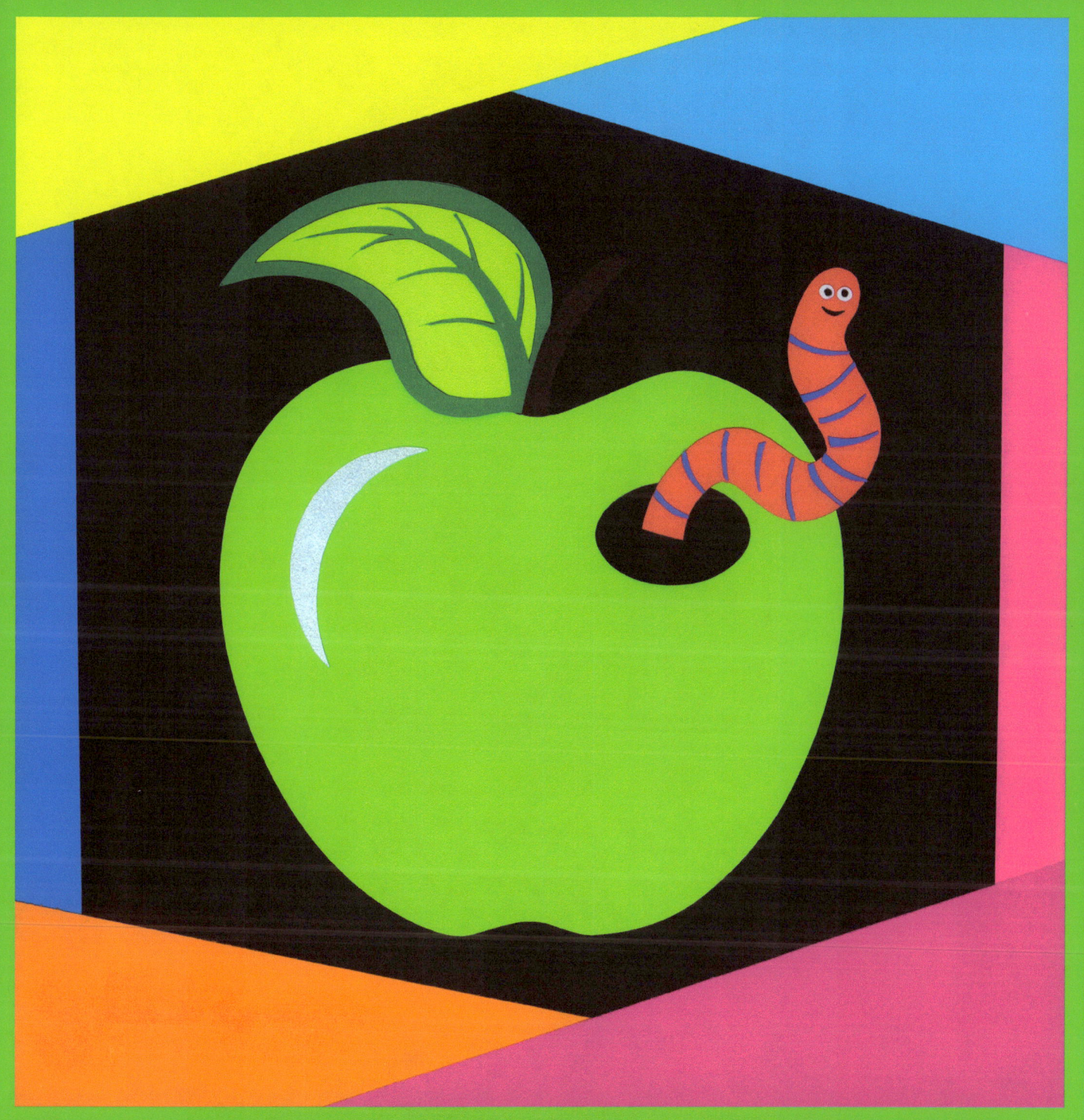

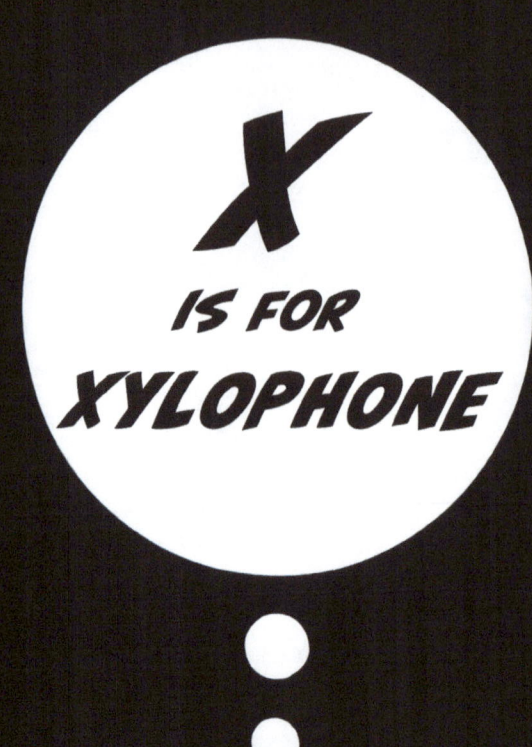

X IS FOR XYLOPHONE

WHICH PAIRS WELL WITH A MICROPHONE!

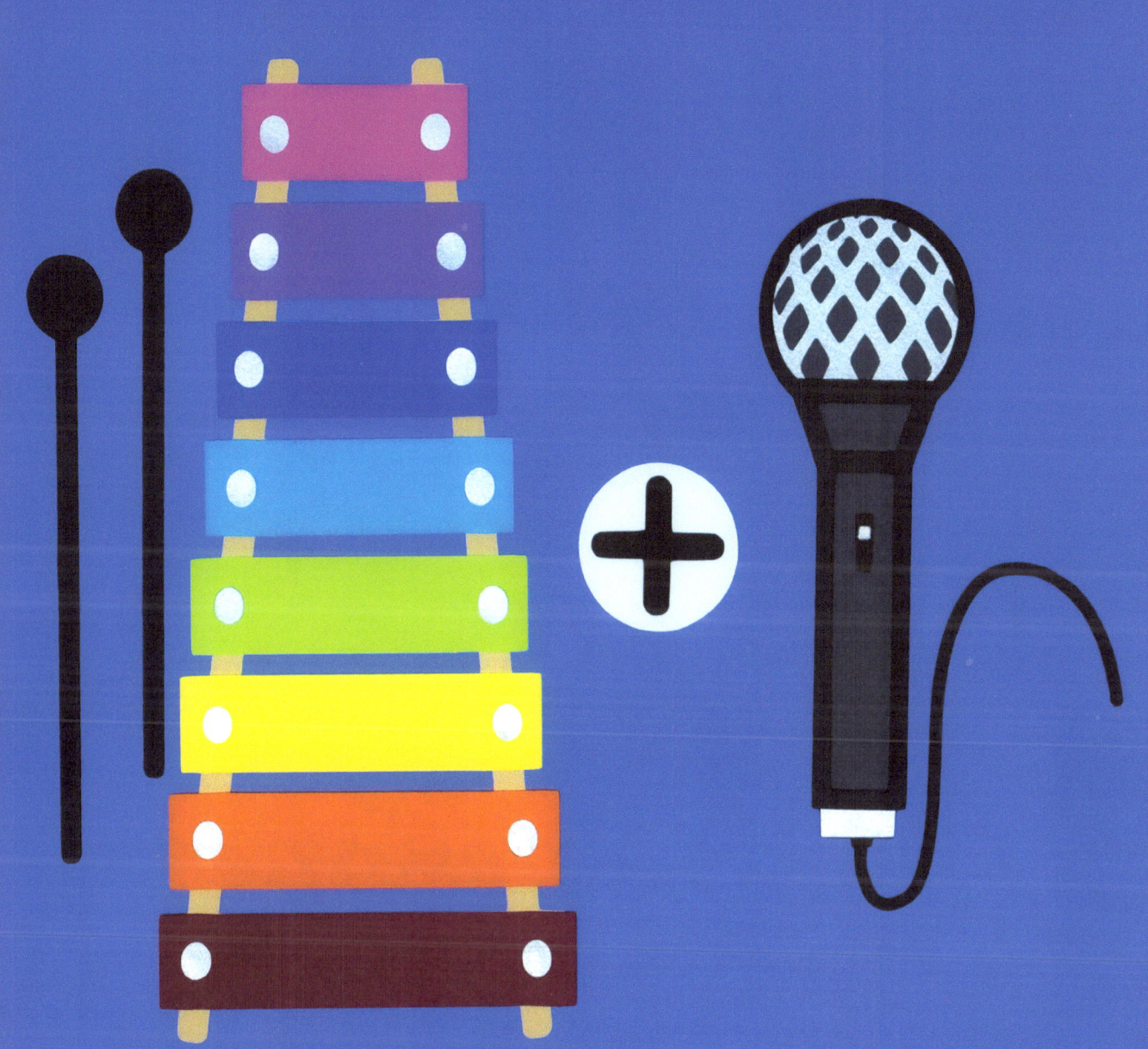

Y
IS FOR
YELLOW

...

LIKE THIS YELLOW CELLO!

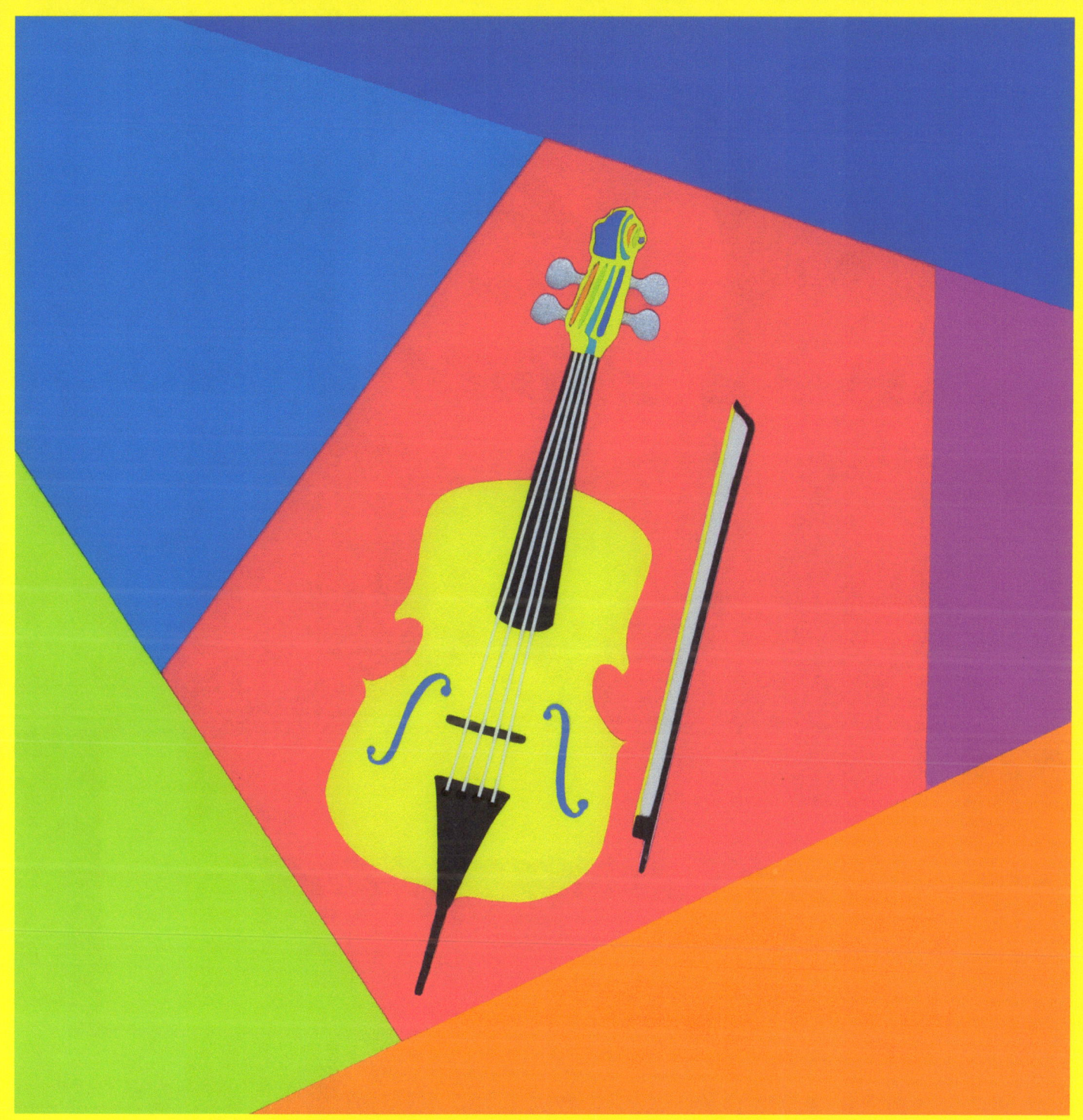

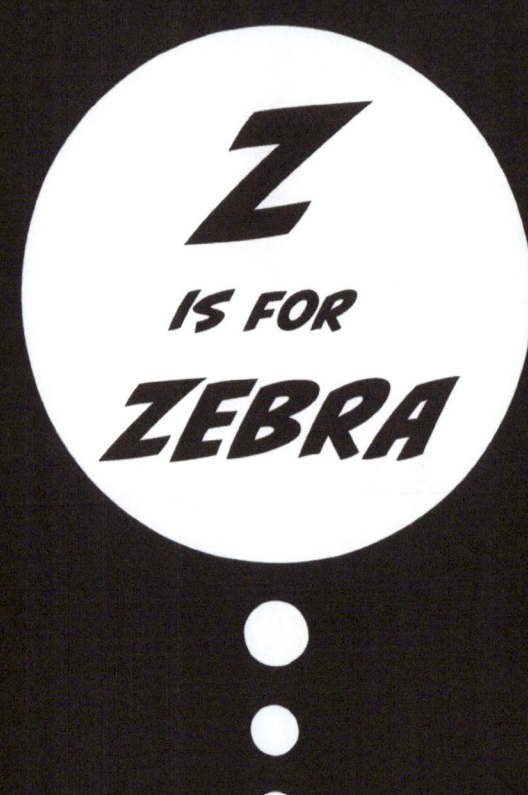

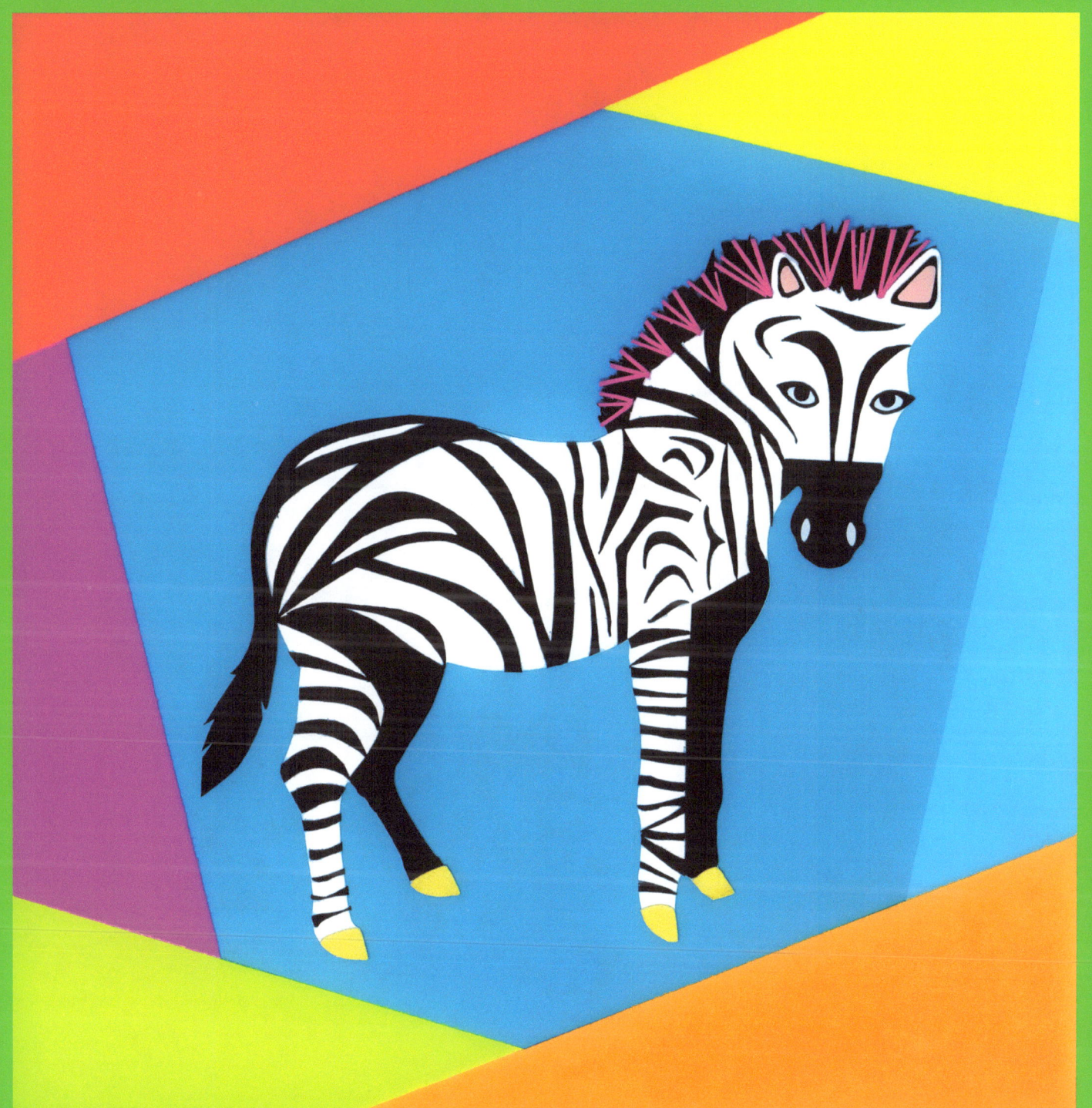

LET'S SAY THE ALPHABET AND RHYME ONE MORE TIME!

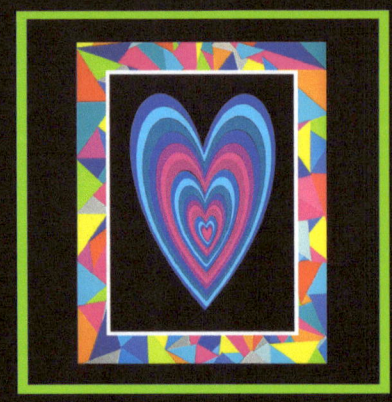

A- ART/HEART

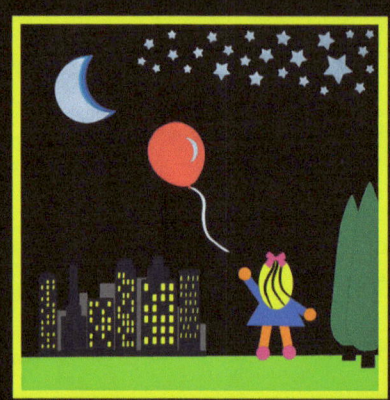

B- BALLOON/MOON

C- CAKE/BAKE

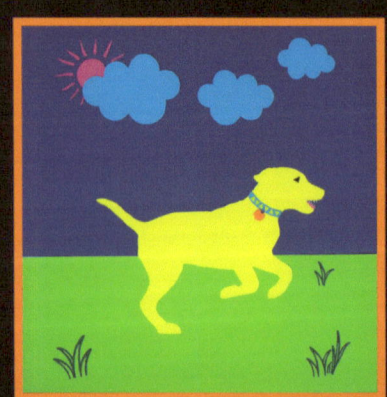

D- DOG/JOG

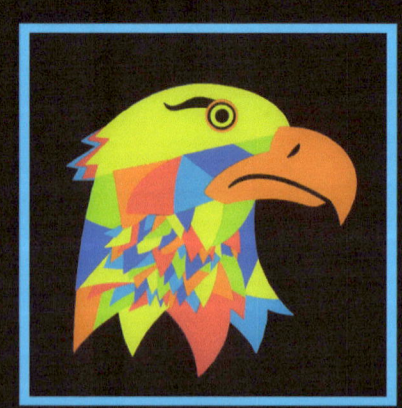

E- EAGLE/REGAL

NICE WORK SAYING A THROUGH E, NOW SAY F THROUGH J WITH ME!

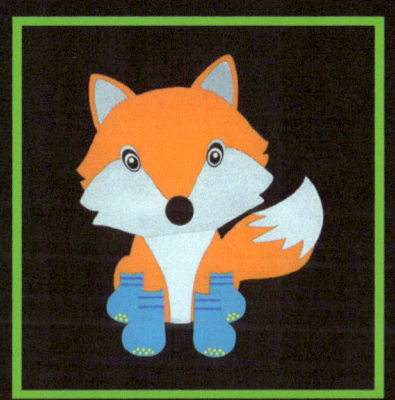

F- FOX/SOCKS

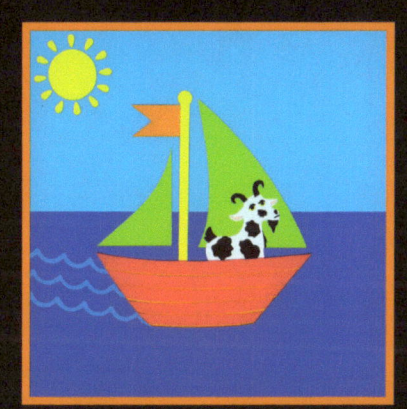

G- GOAT/BOAT

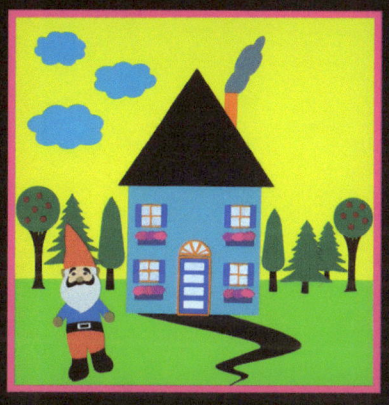

H- HOME/GNOME

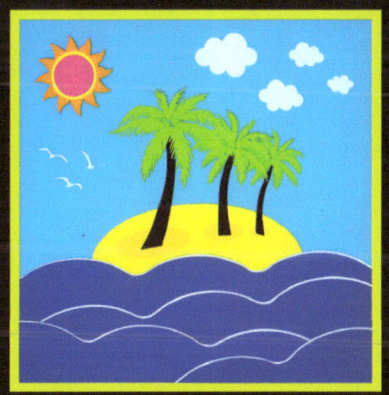

I- ISLAND/"S" SILENT

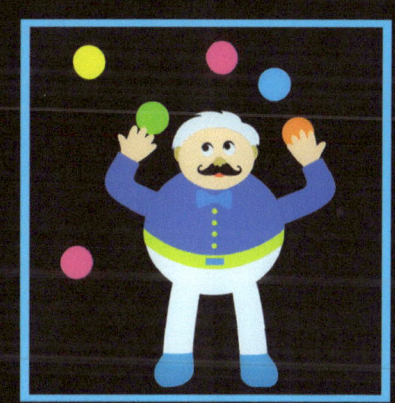

J- JUGGLE/STRUGGLE

NOW ON TO K THROUGH O, THEN ONLY 11 MORE TO GO!

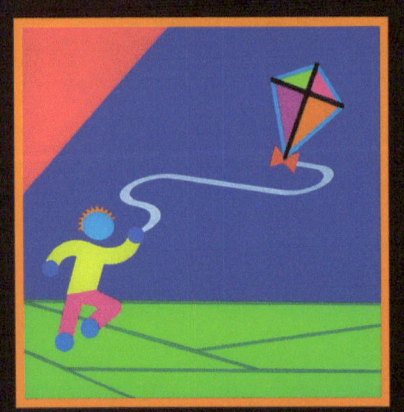
K - KITE/TIGHT

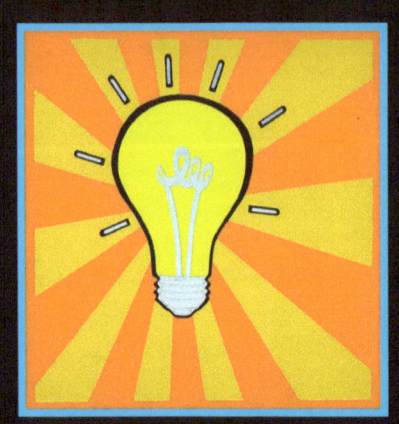
L - LIGHT/BRIGHT

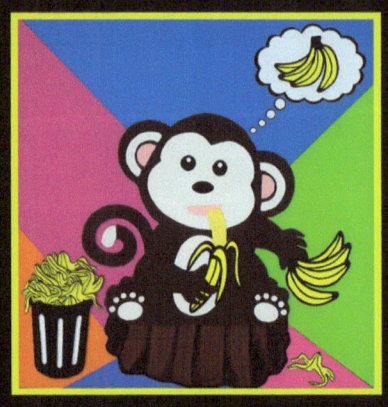
M - MONKEY/JUNKIE

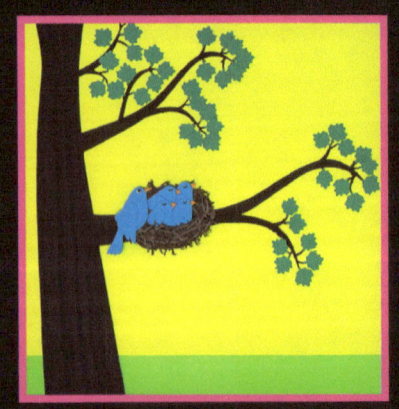
N - NEST/REST

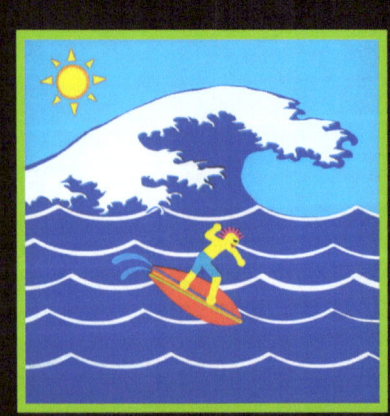
O - OCEAN/MOTION

LOOK AND SEE, YOU'RE ON P THROUGH T!

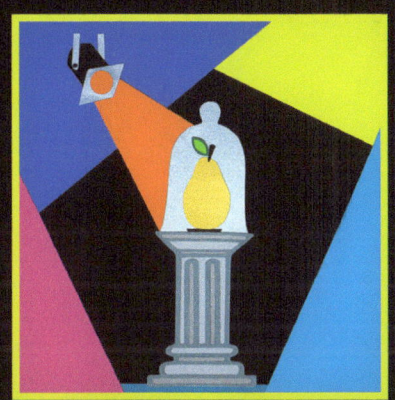

P - PEAR/RARE

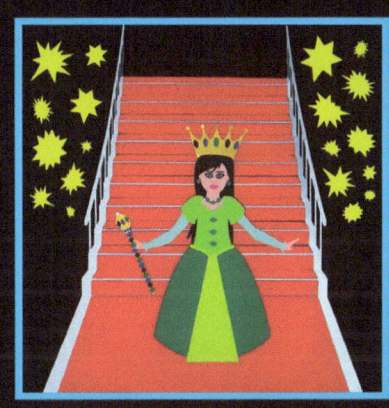

Q - QUEEN/GREEN

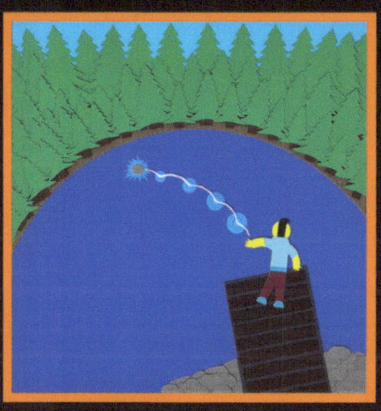

R - ROCK/DOCK

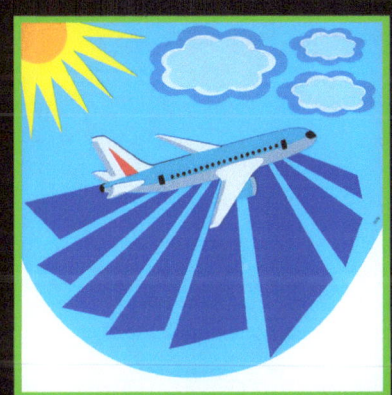

S - SKY/HIGH

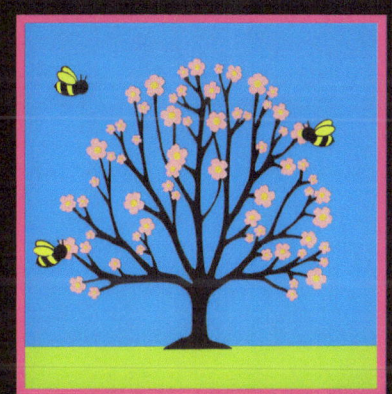

T - TREE/BEES

NOW LET'S FINISH THIS RHYMING SPREE WITH U THROUGH Z!

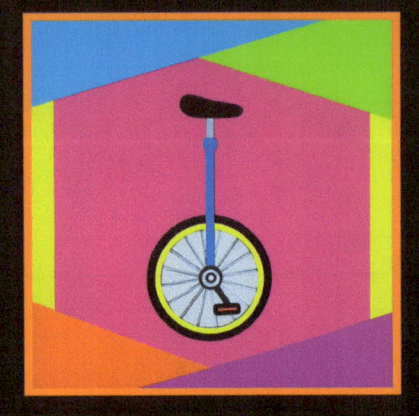
U- UNICYCLE/BICYCLE

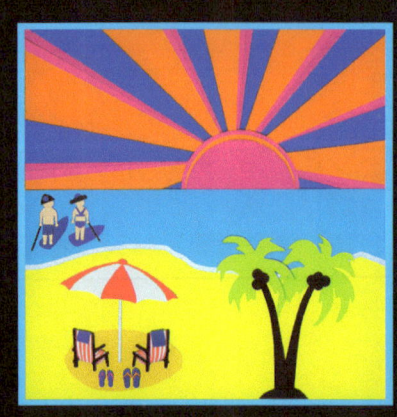
V- VIEW/YOU

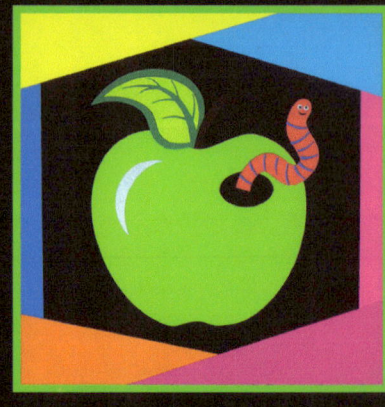
W- WORM/SQUIRM

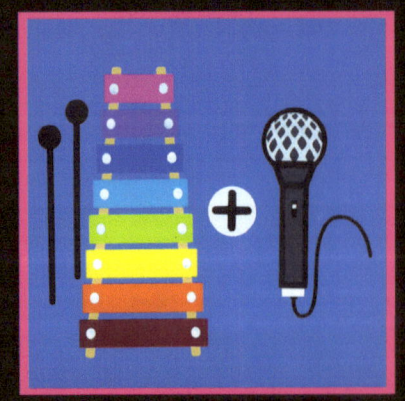
X- XYLOPHONE/MICROPHONE

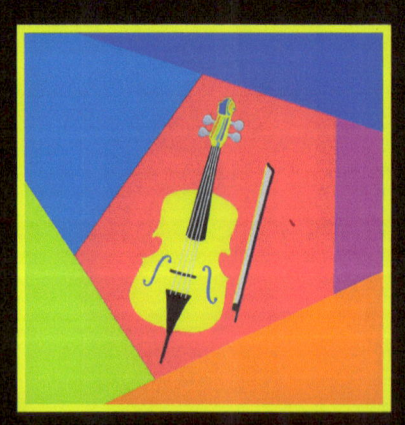
Y- YELLOW/CELLO

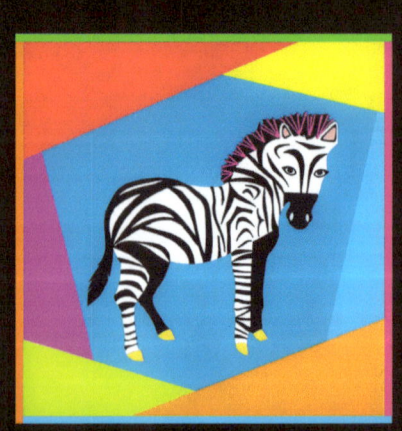
Z- ZEBRA/DIVA

GREAT JOB, AND NOW WE'RE THROUGH.

ISN'T IT FUN TO LEARN SOMETHING NEW!

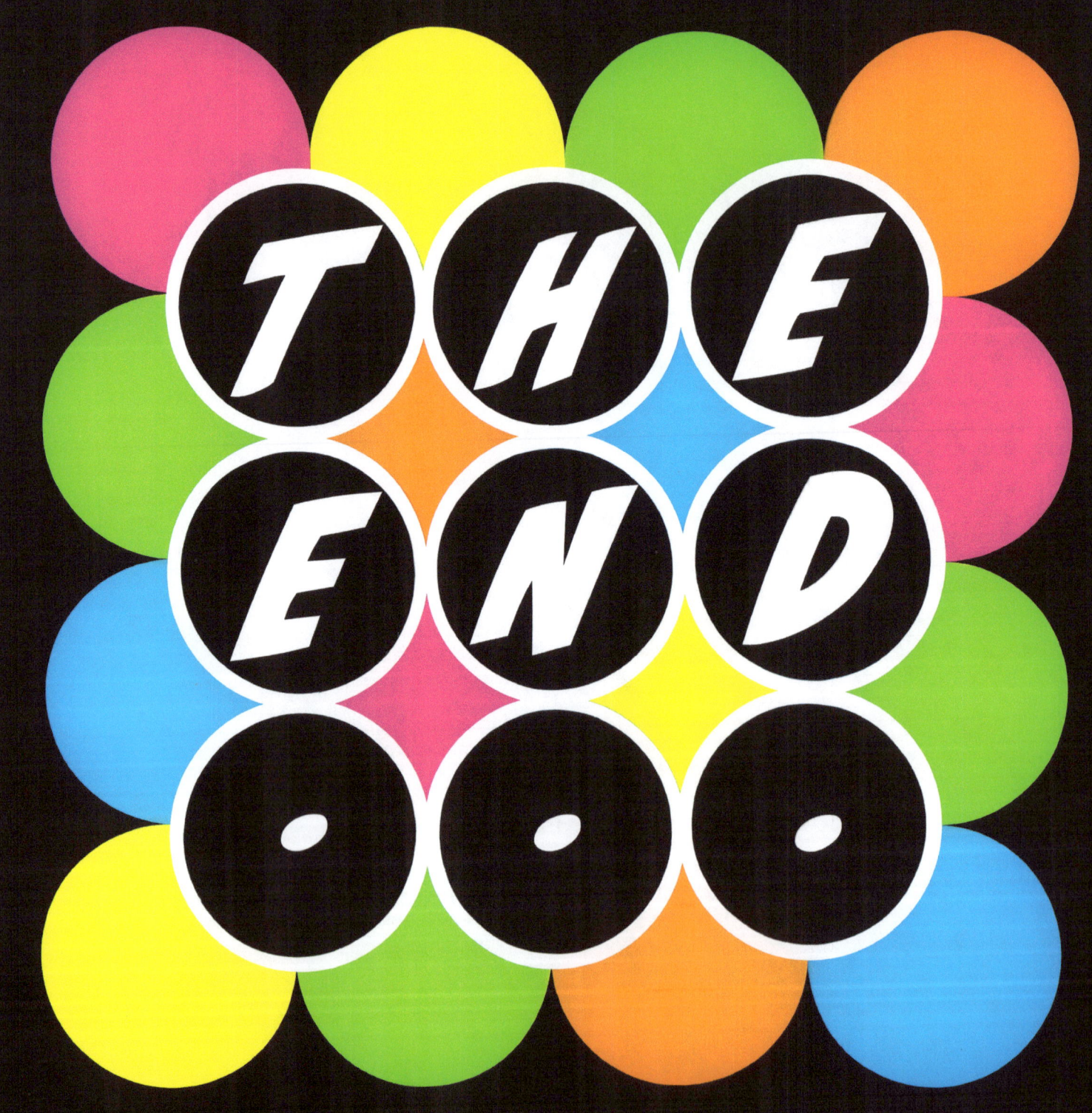

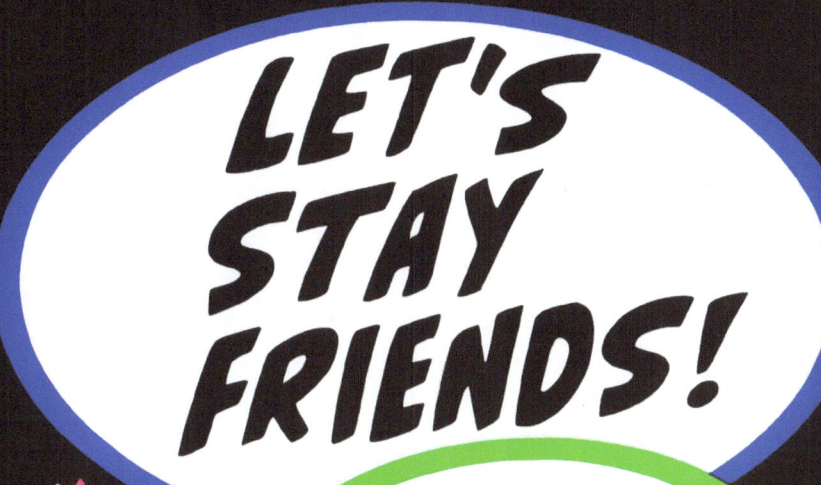

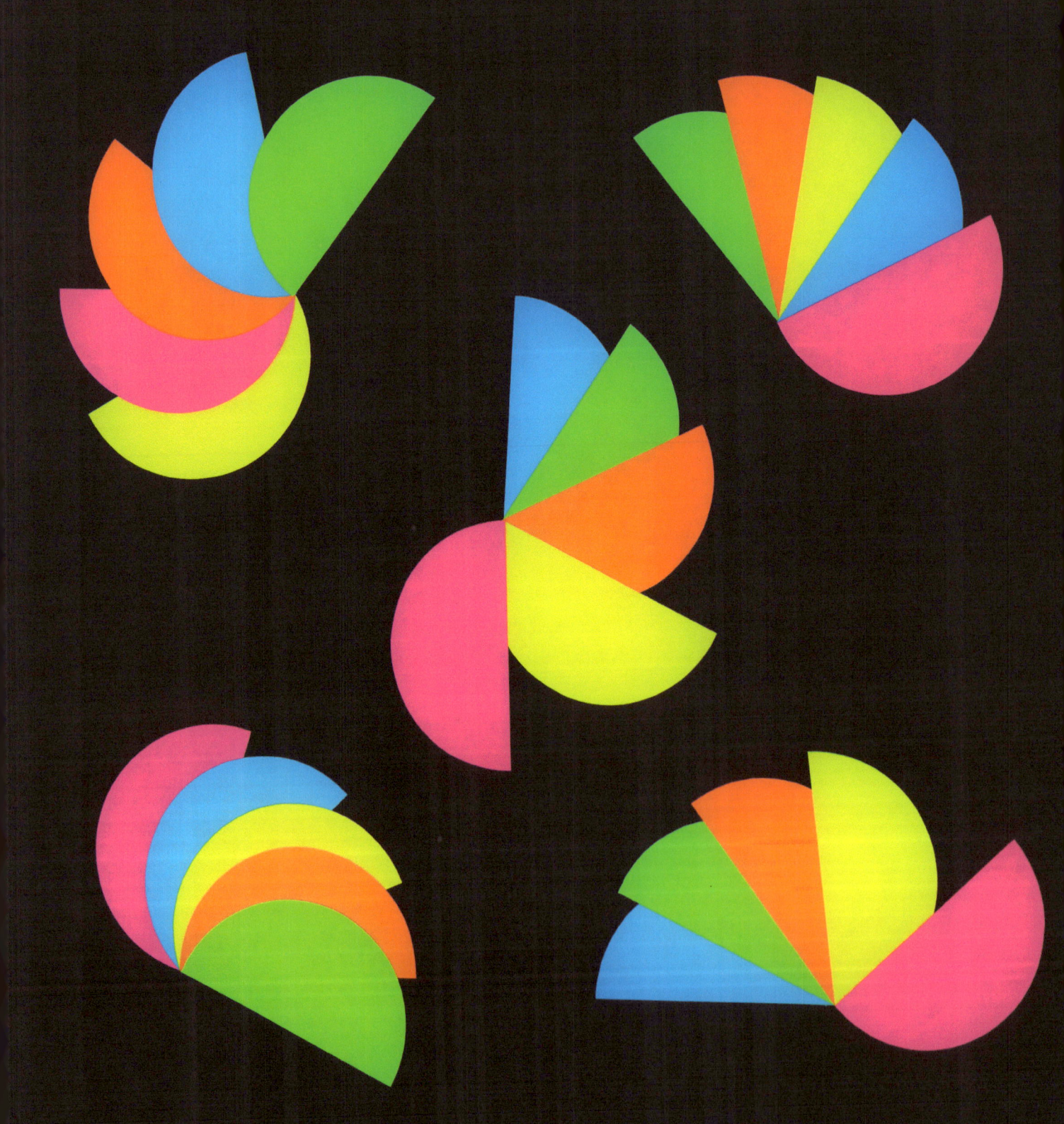

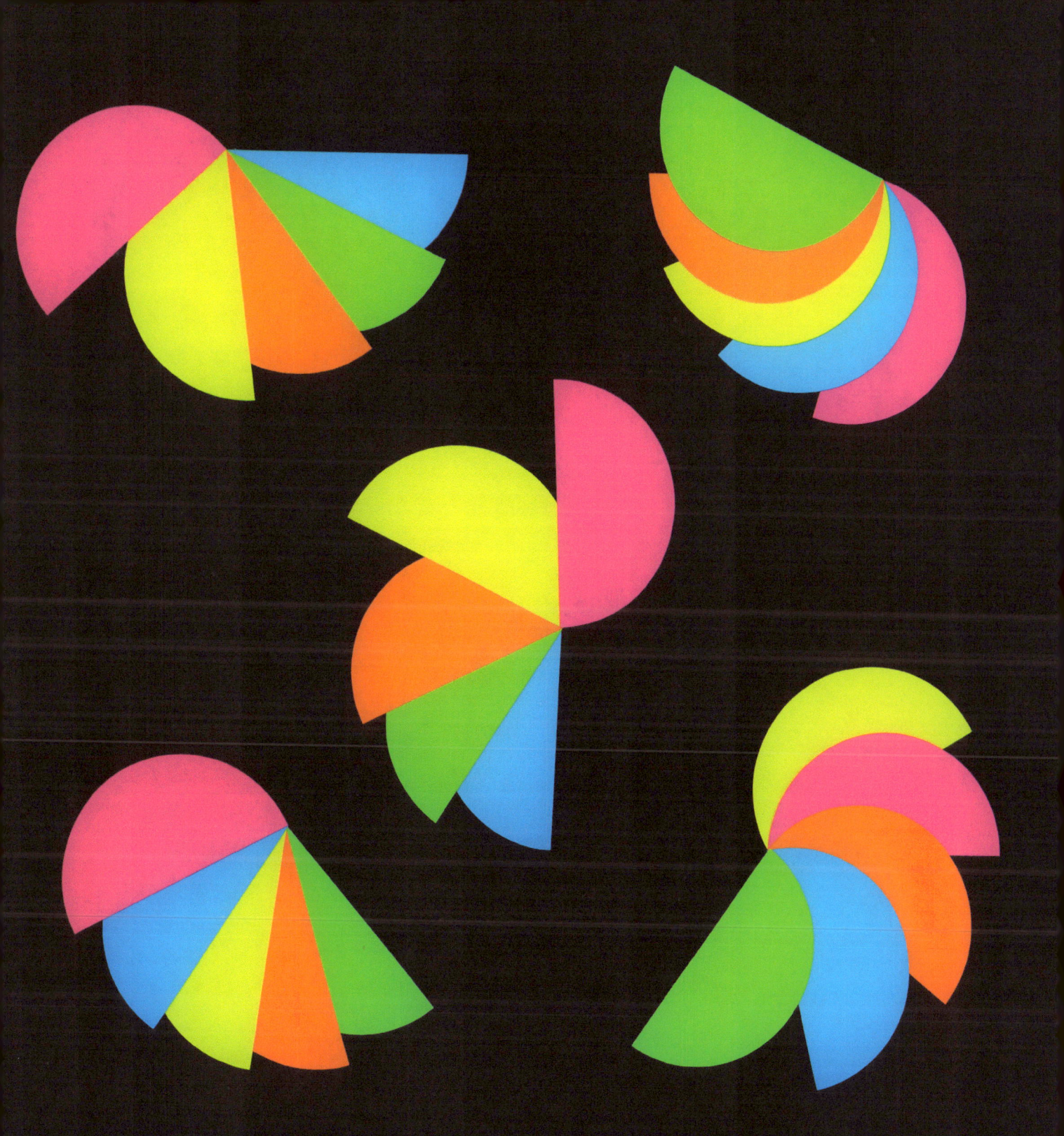

POP ART BOOKs AVAILABLE NOW

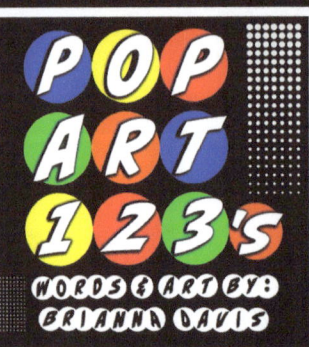
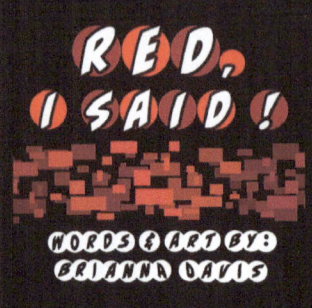
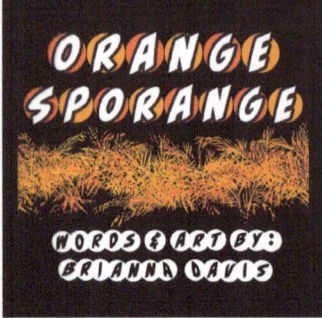
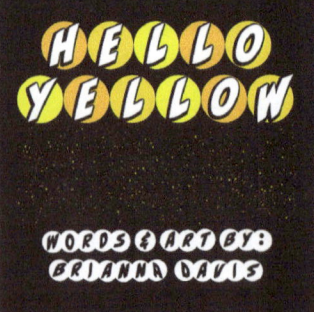
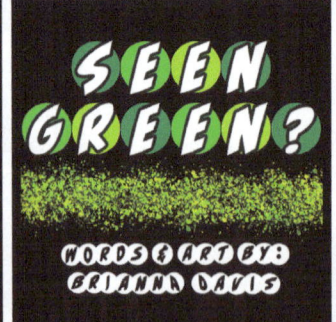
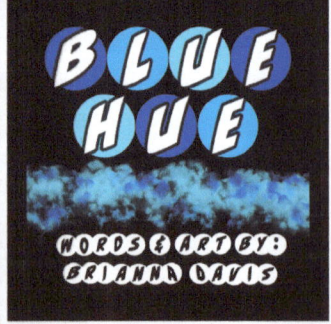
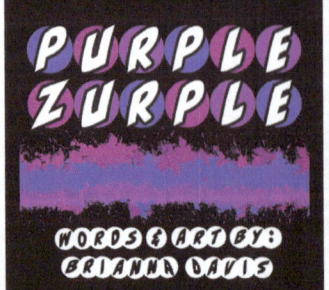
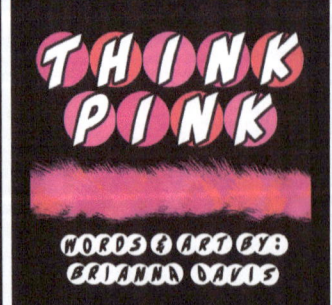
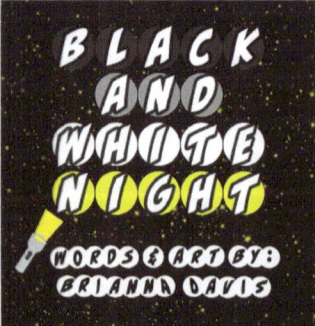

www.ingramcontent.com/pod-product-compliance
Lightning Source LLC
Chambersburg PA
CBHW051204220526
45473CB00003B/894